The Roman Countryside

DUCKWORTH DEBATES IN ARCHAEOLOGY

Series editor: Richard Hodges

Also available

Archaeology and Text
John Moreland

Beyond Celts, Germans and Scythians
Peter S. Wells

Debating the Archaeological Heritage
Robin Skeates

Loot, Legitimacy and Ownership
Colin Renfrew

Origins of the English
Catherine Hills

Towns and Trade in the Age of Charlemagne
Richard Hodges

Villa to Village
Riccardo Francovich & Richard Hodges

The
Roman Countryside

Stephen L. Dyson

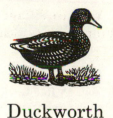

Duckworth

First published in 2003 by
Gerald Duckworth & Co. Ltd.
61 Frith Street, London W1D 3JL
Tel: 020 7434 4242
Fax: 020 7434 4420
inquiries@duckworth-publishers.co.uk
www.ducknet.co.uk

A catalogue record for this book is available
from the British Library

ISBN 0 7156 3225 6

Typeset by Ray Davies
Printed in Great Britain by
Biddles Ltd, *www.biddles.co.uk*

Contents

To students and friends
who have researched the
Roman countryside with me

Introduction

The Roman countryside has been the battleground for much theoretical and ideological debate since the nineteenth century, debates which are still very much alive today. Most had their origins in philological history, although in recent decades they have engaged the world of archaeology. In some instances archaeology has provided important new perspectives and has been used productively. In other cases the evidence of archaeology has been employed selectively to buttress positions based on ideological suppositions and literary sources. The history of these debates is a fascinating one, but beyond my scope here.

In this concise book I set out to describe current research and evaluate discussions on the Roman countryside from a topological rather than a geographical or historical framework. I first examine the Roman villa. Villa studies began in the Renaissance and the villa has ever since remained at the centre of Roman rural studies. I look at changing interpretations of the villa and the ways they have been shaped both by new information and by evolving interpretative models. While I do not make the villa the centrepiece of my own reconstruction of the Roman countryside, I do want to pay proper attention to the mass of information provided by villa archaeology and give due weight to the importance of the villa in Roman rural life.

The second chapter moves from the early history of survey archaeology to its emergence as a major tool for rural settlement reconstruction. Survey has provided much new information not only on villas and farmsteads, but also on other rural economic activities such as pottery production and min-ing. It has also allowed us to reconstruct detailed settlement histories and to appreciate the local and regional variations between different areas of the Roman countryside. I return to some of these themes in the third chapter, where I attempt to relate the survey-settlement evidence to larger questions of landscape use and landscape transformation during the Roman period.

Current interpretative models dealing with the Roman prov-inces stress the degree to which social, cultural, and even economic structures survived from pre-conquest societies, and the importance of active and passive resistance to Roman hegemony. Such approaches are especially important for the countryside. In my fourth chapter I attempt to address some of these issues. I look at provinces such as Sardinia, where long Roman occupation seems to have produced limited changes in rural structures, and areas such as religion, where cultural survivals were especially important. While inherently sympa-thetic to many positions that stress the limits of imperialism, I feel that more emphasis needs to be put on creative synthesis that resulted in new cultural forms.

Archaeologists and historians find it increasingly difficult to describe what happened in rural areas between the end of antiquity and the emergence of medieval society. Archaeology has in recent years provided much new information on this transition. It is clear that the period of transition was much longer than previously thought and that there was tremendous variation, not only between one part of the Empire and another, but between micro-regions within a single province. Here more than elsewhere in this book I can discuss a small sample of recent research projects that provide special new insights into this rapidly changing area of research.

This short work cannot hope to cover all areas of the complex and diverse world of the Roman countryside. It is important that a book on the subject deal with more than just Roman Italy and the Roman Mediterranean. However, space does not allow for a consideration of rural developments throughout the Roman Empire. I submit that the most varied and interesting transformations outside Italy took place in North Africa and in the western provinces. It is also in those areas that some of the most innovative rural research has been conducted. I have therefore decided to focus on Italy, North Africa, the Iberian peninsula, Britain and France within the western Empire.

Italy has to be central, for it was there that the 'Roman countryside' was 'created'. Provence, the Iberian peninsula and North Africa provide good case studies of long periods of Roman rural development where increased social and economic complexity grew out of intense involvement with the Roman market economy. They are all located within the Mediterranean ecological zone and share certain shaping environmental and geographical influences.

Northern France, the Low Countries, Roman Germany and Britain had very different Roman rural histories. They entered into the Roman system late, and had strong indigenous cultures. Certain areas such as the hinterland of the Rhine frontier and the south-east of Britain were strongly transformed by Roman villa culture. In many other regions, however, rural life continued relatively unchanged. Country religion and many aspects of iconography show complex blends of the indigenous and the imperial.

The selection also allows me to draw from very different traditions of archaeological research. Most scholars would agree that Britain and France have surpassed all other regions in the Roman Empire in the intensity and quality of their rural archaeological research. Both have a long and honourable history of antiquarian research, having produced scholars such as Francis Haverfield, Robin Collingwood, Albert Grenier, and Emile Esperandieu, who defined major research paradigms or created invaluable instruments of research. Both were modern imperial powers whose present ideological concerns are reflected in their study of the ancient past. Both countries now have extremely active programmes of public archaeology that each year add massively to our information on the Roman countryside.

Italy and Spain can be described as emerging countries as far as Roman rural archaeology is concerned. Neither country had as strong a rural antiquarian tradition as found in Britain and France, for neither the Italian nor the Spanish educated elite identified with the countryside in the way that the British and French did. Rural archaeological research concentrated on such high-status sites as villas and such elite objects as mosaics. This has changed rapidly in recent years. In both countries public archaeology has become important. Shifts in the ideological orientation of the younger intellectual elites in both Italy and Spain have meant a search for new explanatory frameworks and new research projects. Here the influence of various strands of Marxism has been especially beneficial. The result has been an increased emphasis on problem-oriented archaeology, especially among young scholars who are comfortable using broad-based methods such as field survey that bring into focus the archaeological record of the non-elites.

The complexity of the topic and the compact format of this series have led me to neglect certain important subjects. I have said relatively little about the origins of the Roman countryside. Recent research has demonstrated the complexity of that transition, both in Italy and in the provinces. It should be the theme of yet another volume. I have dealt in only very limited ways with the impact of the military on the rural areas of the Roman Empire. Soldiers were generally recruited from the countryside during both the Republic and the Empire, and in many instances returned there once their military service was completed. During both Republic and Empire supplies were largely drawn from adjacent rural districts. The major frontiers of the West in Britain and Germany were located in rural districts, and they influenced the development of those districts in different ways. I have employed a few examples of intersecting military and rural archaeology, but the topic offers many other possibilities.

My own interest in this subject has been a long one. I first learned provincial archaeology from the late Professor Ian Richmond. My first extensive excavation experience came at the villas of Buccino. I have done survey in both the hinterland of Cosa and the hills of Sardinia. My views on rural history and rural archaeology have been shaped by paradigms as diverse as Gramscian Marxism, the *Gemeinschaft* studies of Ferdinand Tonnies, and the environmentally oriented studies of the historical development of the New England rural landscape. This work, like my earlier study *Community and Society in Roman Italy*, embodies some of my current speculation on this complex phenomenon.

I wish to thank Richard Hodges for inviting me to publish in this series and Deborah Blake for much editorial help. James McCaw prepared the maps. Much help was received from the librarians at the University of Buffalo's Lockwood Library and the library of the American Academy in Rome. I thank my wife Pauline for her help in editing the manuscript. I dedicate it to my students who have helped me explore the Roman countryside over the years.

1

The Roman Villa and the Roman Countryside

The Renaissance humanists sought to connect the classical past with their contemporary world in many and diverse ways. Some attempted to associate the surviving remains of Roman villas with famous owners known through literary texts, giving a major stimulus to the discipline of Roman rural archaeology. Others combined philology and archaeology to recreate the villa as both ideal type and real structure. Their efforts stimulated a whole range of humanistic activities from architecture to agriculture.

Roman authors, especially Cicero and Pliny, provided not only an excellent general picture of the importance of villa culture for the life of the Roman elite in the later Republic and early Empire, but also specific information on the design and operation of their own villas and those of their friends. Cicero's Tusculan villa was the setting of some of his most important writings, and in his letters he said much about the suburban and country residences of friends. Horace waxed eloquent on the delights of his Sabine villa. Pliny the Young wrote extensively on villa architecture and lifestyle.

Renaissance humanists and antiquarians attempted to match these accounts with rural ruins, particularly those that dotted the Alban hills. These hills, with their cool pleasant settings and easy access to Rome, attracted the Renaissance nobility, both clerical and secular, as they had once attracted the ancient Roman senatorial and imperial elite. Elegant villas were built at places like Frascati near ancient Tusculum where Cicero had lived. Humanists began exploring the ruined villa platforms in the surrounding hills and trying to associate them with places mentioned in the classical sources. Names such as the Villa of Cicero and the Villa of Lucullus appeared on those first archaeological maps. Much scholarly debate has ensued over the centuries, and it is unlikely that we will ever be able to associate most rural ruins with the country homes of famous Romans with any degree of probability. However, even today maps of places like Tivoli and the Bay of Naples identify villa remains with specific Roman owners.

The Younger Pliny's detailed descriptions of his Tuscan and Laurentine villas provide detailed information on villa construction, organization and usage that became points of reference both for those attempting to recreate the lifestyle of the Romans and for those seeking to reconstruct the physical appearance of the villas from the exiguous archaeological remains. Over the centuries many attempts, both verbal and visual, have been made to recreate the architecture of Pliny's villas. A competition for the most imaginative reconstruction of Pliny's Laurentine Villa was held as late as the early 1980s, demonstrating the grip that Pliny's descriptions have maintained on the post-Renaissance architectural imagination (Culot & Pinon 1982; DuPrey 1994).

The Renaissance also saw efforts to create a new country lifestyle based in part on the revival of Roman villa rituals. For the first time since the collapse of the Roman Empire, an urban elite made substantial investments in rural dwellings designed for more than defence and agricultural productivity. The virtues of Cato were not forgotten, but the new elite also wished to practise the rustic liberal arts of Cicero or Pliny the Younger in an appropriate setting. Such neo-Roman rural worlds emerged first around Florence and Rome. However, the most concentrated expression of cultured rustication was created during the sixteenth century in the Veneto. There, in the newly developed

1. The Roman Villa and the Roman Countryside

Terra Firma of the declining Venetian Republic, the architect Andrea Palladio designed a great number of elegant villas reflecting strong classical influences. Palladio had read his Vitruvius, and knew what that author and other ancients regarded as the elements that should be incorporated into a villa. Buildings such as his Villa Rotondo near Vicenza were more than just embodiments of antiquarian good taste. They were also expressions of 'hegemonic architecture' – the use of impressive buildings to enhance the elite's social and political control of the countryside (Bentmann & Muller 1992). This was especially important in the world of sixteenth-century Venice, for this new rural nobility often did not have deep feudal roots in the Terra Firma. Their classicizing villas emphasized the appropriate historical associations and reinforced the right to rule that came with cultural superiority.

The eighteenth century saw the rise of a new country gentry and nobility, particularly in England. Educated in the Classics and familiar through the Grand Tour with both the Roman ruins of Italy and the classically inspired villas of Palladio, these British noblemen, beginning with Lord Burlington (1694-1753), graced their native landscape with elegant country houses that reflected both the inspiration of Palladio and a desire to emulate Romans such as Cicero and Pliny. The first book in English on Roman villas, Robert Castell's *The Villas of the Ancients*, was published in 1728 (DuPrey 1994: 131-42). Behind what might be called the 'whig' ideology of these new British country houses was a strong sense of identification with the Roman Republic. Country members of parliament saw themselves as reviving the values of republican Rome and opposing the despotic regimes of the European continent.

The Augustan Age of eighteenth-century England also brought another famous Roman villa-owner to the fore. Horace, the favourite Latin poet of the age, had received a Sabine villa from his patron Maecenas and celebrated its charms in his poems. His country house, as he described it, was not a grandiose place but a modest, comfortable abode. Horace's description of his Sabine pleasures provided a model of civilized leisure (*otium*) for a range of educated Englishmen whose economic and social status placed them well below the owners of 'stately homes'. This passion for the rustic Horace stimulated another fashion in archaeological tourism as enthusiastic Englishmen sought the site of his villa. By the later eighteenth century, many antiquarians had agreed on a location near the Sabine town of Vicovaro, which Horace-lovers made into a place of regular pilgrimage. By the nineteenth century so many British citizens had passed through Vicovaro that the local peasantry had come to think that Horace was an Englishman (Frischer & Brown 2001). Excavation in the early twentieth century unearthed a villa complex whose date and location fitted Horace's Sabine farm, but whose remains were considerably more extensive and elegant than the poet's descriptions implied (Lugli 1926).

That vision of a revived Roman countryside was carried to America, where it underwent further mutations. Thomas Jefferson with his Palladian-inspired villa on the mountaintop at Monticello best represents the ideals of Roman country *otium* carried to America (Lehmann 1991). However, since the country house had also become identified with corrupt and despotic qualities of the British nobility, it had to be refashioned for post-Revolutionary America. More acceptable was an association with the rural world of early Rome which another Virginia planter, George Washington, identified with Cincinnatus, the man who left his plough and his modest plantation at Mount Vernon to save the Republic. Ironically this country world of the new Cincinnatus was also one based on slavery (Wills 1984).

Starting in the eighteenth century, ancient Roman villa sites became the object of more systematic topographical and later archaeological explorations. Hadrian's Villa at Tivoli had interested antiquarians and architects since the Renaissance, when Pirro Ligorio studied its ruins while supervising the design and construction of the nearby Villa d'Este. By the eighteenth century Hadrian's Villa had become more of a mine for art objects that could be sold to Englishmen visiting Italy (MacDonald & Pinto 1995). The discovery and excavation of the luxurious Villa of the Papyri at Herculaneum during that period provided a new, very complete picture of Roman villa life (Parslow 1995). Large quantities of sculpture were recovered as well as charred papyri with the writings of the first century BC Epicurean philosopher Philodemos. The owner was probably L. Calpurnius Piso, father-in-law of Julius Caesar. Located on the Bay of Naples, the playground of the late Republican aristocracy, the Villa of the Papyri came to embody the cultivated if decadent *otium* of the age of Caesar. Appropriately, the American oil tycoon and art collector John Paul Getty used the Villa of the Papyri as the model for his classical art museum at Malibu, California.

Interest in the Roman villa was further stimulated by excavations undertaken by amateur archaeologists, especially in Britain and France. While the English country nobility went on the Grand Tour and collected classical art for their Neo-Palladian residences, the local gentry and clergy, also educated in the Classics, created their own archaeology through the exploration of the remains of the Roman provincial villas that dotted the European countryside. During the late eighteenth and early nineteenth centuries the rural landscape of England in particular was transformed as agricultural production intensified, canals were dug, and railroads built. Those development projects unearthed many Roman archaeological remains, especially villa sites. The villa ruins made for ideal excavations in that era of amateur archaeology. Most were located away from rapidly developing urban areas and lent themselves to the leisurely pace that characterized Victorian archaeology. Many were on private property and thus enjoyed special protection by the laws and customs of English rural society. When one season was finished the diggers could look forward to the site being intact the next year. Many yielded substantial remains such as baths and mosaics. Occasionally the excavations yielded more spectacular finds such as a hoard of coins or silver plate left behind as the owners fled some barbarian attack. While the study of Roman pottery was still in its infancy, Roman coins could be dated and the villa site placed in some kind of historical context.

The antiquarians recorded these discoveries in their diaries, reported on them at their local learned society meetings, and published the results in their local newspapers and periodicals. Decades of patient research by our often forgotten scholarly forebears laid the foundations for the Roman rural archaeology that we still use today. It also made the villa even more central to the understanding of the dynamics of Roman country life. There was also forged a further sense of identity between Roman past and British present, for these rural parsons and country gentry liked to think of themselves as the spiritual if not literal descendents of the Romans who had brought civilized life to rural France and England.

For much of the twentieth century the ideology and even the methods of villa archaeology remained basically the same, as can be seen in the excavation of the Villa of the Mysteries, just outside the gates of Pompeii. Part of the villa, including the room with the 'Mysteries' wall-paintings showing some type of Dionysiac female ritual, had been discovered in 1909-10. In 1929-30 Amadeo Maiuri returned to the site, clearing the rest of the central structure and undertaking the repairs and restorations that would make the site accessible to the public. Maiuri's numerous publications reveal interesting insights into his own villa ideology. A conservative Catholic who supported Mussolini, he saw in the paintings the type of spiritual elevation that one would expect from cultivated Roman *otium*. Maiuri did unearth some sections of the *pars rustica*, or rural processing unit, of the Villa of the Mysteries. He interpreted those as the additions of new business-based owners, whose new commercial vulgarity was in the process of effacing surviving traces of the refined lifestyle of the earlier owners when the eruption of AD 79 destroyed the villa.

Villa studies have formed a central part of the archaeology of the Roman countryside for over five hundred years. We have more information about the Roman villa than we do about any other Roman architectural form. A recent gazetteer of Roman villas in Britain (E. Scott 1993) listed over two thousand for that province alone. Jean-Gerard Gorges, operating with a much less extensive archaeological database, has documented hundreds in the Iberian peninsula (Gorges 1979). These figures are worth keeping in mind when I consider recent arguments for the limits of Romanization. Our information on villas covers in detail all of the areas of the Empire under consideration in this study. That cannot be said of the archaeological survey data, and certainly not of the background environmental information.

The next question is what we do with such material. The first problem is a semantic one. The ancient authors themselves lumped under the designation 'villa' a range of rural structures. The modern archaeological term 'villa' has been used to describe a variety of buildings, from modest country houses with small baths and a few luxury furnishings to grand imperial residences. More architectural, social and economic precision is needed in defining the rural structures designated as villas. That is a topic to which I will return. It is also important to bear in mind the uneven quality of our archaeological information. Very few villas were excavated under scientific archaeological conditions even for their time, and even fewer using methods that would be acceptable today. Publication has been patchy. Most of what has been recovered and published consists of plans, mosaics and sculpture. What can this defective but cumulatively massive evidence tell the archaeologist of the early twenty-first century?

The key message is the enormous influence that the Roman

villa as both an architectural form and a social and economic structure had on the western Mediterranean and the European countryside from the late second century BC to the fourth/fifth century AD. While displaying considerable variety in size, scale and detail, most shared certain core qualities that expressed the values of 'Roman country gentlemen'. Probably no other building form and cultural institution has had such an influence before or since, other than perhaps the monastery. The medieval monastery indeed makes an interesting comparison with the villa because it was both an institution and a structure and displayed considerable variation in detail while sharing core elements that are the expressive of its overall shaping ideology.

The classification of villas is a complex and much debated subject. The long tradition of villa archaeology has provided much information on the plans of villas, most of them fragmentary, but some relatively complete. Our information is weighted of favour of the residential unit, the so-called *pars urbana*, over the *pars rustica*, the agricultural working area of the villa, for the former was more likely to yield impressive architecture, mosaics and sculpture. Until recently, archaeologists displayed only limited interest in the productive side of the villa, but this has changed with both the emergence of Marxist models of Roman rural life and the increasing ability of archaeologists to extract more information from environmental data and objects of ordinary life.

Many different classifactory schemes have been employed to bring order and meaning to this inchoate architectural information. The usefulness and problems of some of these schemes will be discussed in later contexts. As a starter, a brief discussion of the three major geographical/functional divisions of *villa maritima*, *villa suburbana*, and *villa rustica* can provide an introduction to this most distinctive architectural form in Roman rural life.

Possibly the most innovative, and from an elite social point of view the most important, of the villa types was the *villa maritima*. Starting in the late second century BC, senators and wealthy equestrians constructed luxury villas along the Italian coast, especially in the zone between Rome and the Bay of Naples. At almost every scenic point along that beautiful stretch of the Mediterranean, remains of major Roman villas have been documented. Some were modest buildings, but many were large and ornate, for the Roman elite used the shoreline of Italy as an architectural exercise in conspicuous consumption. Two of the most famous villas, the Villa of the Papyri at Herculaneum and the Villa of Tiberius at Sperlonga, belong to that category. Pliny the Younger was a member of the imperial maritime villa set, and his letter describing his villa at Laurentum south of Rome provides our most detailed description of such a villa and what it meant to the owner. Pliny's villa was hardly unique in that area, and indeed the coastal road south of Ostia was lined with sumptuous residences, like a modern seaside development. So closely packed were the villas that the ancients described the view as more like a packed cityscape than a rustic perspective.

Most of these *villae maritimae* are today only picturesque ruins. Few have been excavated, and even fewer have been excavated well. The emphasis has generally been on the reconstruction of the plans and architectural histories of the complexes and the recovery of decorative objects. A good example of the latter are the sculptural groups depicting scenes from the adventures of Odysseus that were discovered at the Villa of Tiberius at Sperlonga shortly after World War II. However, this jumble of archaeological information related to the maritime villa contains much that is useful. Xavier Lafon has recently (2001) gathered together much of this material and provided an historical synthesis that demonstrates not only the cultural but also the socio-economic importance of the *villa maritima* for the Roman western Mediterranean.

While the research emphasis, both archaeological and historical, has been on the maritime villa as an institution of high culture (D'Arms 1970), archaeologists have been increasingly interested in investigating the *partes rusticae* of these seaside villas and reconstructing their economic functions and the ways they contributed to the income of the elite. Economically as well as visually, *villae maritimae* formed a link between the sea-shore and the countryside. Their owners owned and managed an extensive retro-terra that produced agricultural products for export, and these were shipped out through the small ports or roadsteads that the villa-owners often controlled. That seems to have been the case with the isolated maritime villa at Sarpi in the Gulf of Polikastro south of Naples and with a number of villas along the Calabrian coast. The owners of maritime villas were often involved in fishing, fish-farming, and fish-process-ing, especially those used for the production of *garum* (fish sauce). This aspect of maritime villa life has been well docu-mented along the south and west coasts of Spain and Portugal, where many of the elite residences produced evidence for fish-processing and for the manufacture of the amphorae used as containers in the long-distance shipping of *garum*. The presence of such noxious activities so close to the summer retreats of the elite is a reminder of the economic role that almost all villas played, and of the importance of commerce in the maintenance of the lifestyle of the upper strata of Roman society.

The harbour of the Roman colony of Cosa provides good documentation for such seaside production and shipping asso-ciated with the activities of the villa economy. The Romans had invested considerably in the improvement of the Cosan road-stead in order to provide a better harbour for the colony and its hinterland (McCann *et al.* 1987). However, by the early to middle first century BC the colony was in decline and the little harbour was increasingly used to serve the needs of the major families whose great villas had come to dominate the surround-ing countryside. During those years the senatorial family of the Sestii established an amphora production facility at the harbour to provide shipping containers for their widely distributed vintages. Then, or only slightly later, a large villa maritima was built on the harbour. Later, under the Empire, an extensive fish-breeding facility was constructed nearby. Other smaller harbour communities may have experienced similar developments. Amphora production was so massive at the northern Campanian coastal city of Sinuessa that sherds and wasters were used as construction material.

The other two important types of villas were the *villa suburbana* and the *villa rustica*. The suburban villa, as the name implies, was a country residence located close to a city or town. It allowed the proprietor to participate fully in town political and social life, while enjoying some of the *otium* associated with country life, exercising tighter control over his rural economic interests, and enjoying greater flexibility in architectural design than was possible in the crowded cities and towns. All the roads leading out of Rome were lined with such structures, as the remains of such massive suburban complexes as the Villa of Maxentius and the Villa of the Quintilii attest. However, not all the suburban villas were grandiose, and we now have considerable evidence for smaller suburban structures whose owners profited from the complex market-garden demands of the capital. The two villas on the Via Gabina excavated by Rice University belong in that category. They had long histories of occupation and combined modest comforts with agricultural production facilities. The Villa of the Mysteries at Pompeii represents the same phenomenon in the context of a smaller community. While suburban villas have taught us much about the architectural and artistic taste of the Roman and small town elites, their economic roles have not received the attention they deserve.

The 'true *villa rustica*' tended to be located away from the coast and away from the major urban centers, although few were far removed from any *colonia* or *municipium*. They are the spiritual and, to a certain degree, the functional ancestors of eighteenth/nineteenth-century English country houses. The best literary account that we have of the form and function of the larger *villa rustica* is Pliny's description of his residence in the upper Tiber valley. They vary considerably in plan, scale and occupation history. While the initial framework of our understanding of these villas comes from the antiquarian literature, recent archaeological research has massively increased our knowledge of their nature and history. It is the *villa rustica* that will provide many of the examples I will use in describing other aspects of Roman rural life.

The survival of the decorative elements of villas, such as sculpture and mosaics, stimulated early antiquarian interest in their archaeology. The writings of Pliny and especially Cicero show the care that villa-owners took in decorating their villas and ordering sculptural originals and copies to suit particular contexts. However, it is almost impossible to find a villa with all its furnishings and decorations intact. Even at the Villa of the Papyri, destroyed in AD 79, archaeologists have determined that the owners were still in the process of rebuilding after a recent earthquake, and that many of the sculptures were not in their original locations, making the task of reconstructing the programmatic intentions of that particular owner-collector more difficult. Most villas have been almost totally looted. However a few, such as that at Chiragan in the Pyrenees, have yielded quantities of high quality sculpture that allow the reconstruction of the changing values and tastes of the owners. Good fortune has led to the recovery of other furnishings. In a number of instances caches of gold and silver plate have been found at villas, buried and forgotten as the owners fled some disasters. Many are late in date and provide insight into the survival of not only an elegant lifestyle but also a pagan worldview, at a time when Roman culture was being transformed by both Christian and barbarian.

Villa walls, like those of urban residences, were elaborately decorated The painted decoration of such Pompeian rural residences as the Villa of the Mysteries and Villas at Boscoreale and Boscotrecase have long been known. More recent excavations in the Neapolitian suburbs produced a spectacular series of paintings in the *villa maritima* of ancient Oplontis. Improved excavation techniques at villa excavations such as that at Settefinestre near Cosa have led to the recovery of sufficient quantities of painted plaster to allow the reconstruction of the decorative schemes. Each year more is learned about villa painting in both Italy and the provinces, but our information on that medium is still very incomplete.

Floor mosaics have provided the most abundant and diverse information on many artistic and cultural aspects of Roman villa life. Set in hard Roman cement and often deeply buried in the debris of the collapsing buildings, they have proved very durable, surviving centuries of abuse by the elements and agricultural activities. The rural areas of Italy, North Africa, Iberia, France and Britain have yielded tens of thousands of Roman mosaics, and more are constantly being discovered. They were the products of craft workshops that employed a wide-ranging iconography and operated at a great range of technical levels, and they represent one of the most important expressions of Roman consumer culture. Almost every relatively prosperous villa-owner could afford at least one mosaic. Most used only geometric patterns, but others depict complex scenes drawn from classical myth and literature. Some were executed with great care and great subtlety of coloration and representation of perspective. Others, like those from villas located on the fringe areas of Romanized Britain, were the works of craftsmen only marginally acquainted with classical craft traditions.

Like the villas themselves, the mosaics represent one of our largest bodies of information on elite Roman rural life. They can be approached in a variety of ways. The high culture oriented art historian seeks from them information on lost works of Greek and Roman painters or on the general parameters of elite taste. Since many mosaics were placed in residential entertainment areas, they fit in well with growing interest in the rituals of Roman dining. Other subject themes provide information on such topics as rural architecture in North Africa and the games of the amphitheatre. Even the crudest pictorial mosaics have their value, for they provide information on the intersection of high classical and popular art and the survival of pre-Roman representational traditions even among the Romanized rural elites of the provinces.

Detailed stylistic and technical analyses have allowed art historians to reconstruct the general history of mosaic representation and even to identify regional schools of mosaic workers, whether the high-end North African craftsmen who worked at the sumptuous late Antique African and Sicilian villas or the more humble craftsmen who decorated the villas of south-western Britain in the fourth century AD. The former school is best represented at the opulent fourth-century villa found at Piazza Armerina in central Sicily. The extremely complex mosaics installed there employed themes ranging from classical mythology to the delights of the hunt and the bedroom, and captured the wide-ranging ideological vision of its senatorial owner. The reconstruction of the Romano-British school not only demonstrated the survival of elite values well into the fourth century, but also the shift of the epicenter of rural prosperity from south-east to south-west England.

Architectural plans, sculptures, mosaics and other objects recovered from the many excavations in the countryside from the Renaissance to the present must play an important role in our reconstruction of Roman rural life. However, they are no substitute for the diverse range of information that can be recovered from a high quality modern villa excavation that employs not only the best field technicians, but also the full range of experts who can extract data from the great body of artifactual and environmental material recovered. In recent years an increasing number of these high quality excavations have been carried out, first in northern provincial areas such as Britain and Germany, and then in Italy itself. Only a handful of these excavations can be considered in a short work like this.

Possibly the most influential villa excavation during the past generation was that undertaken during the 1970s by an Anglo-Italian team at the luxurious villa of Settefinestre near Cosa. The ruins were those of a multi-terraced rural residence that appears to have been built in the first century BC and to have gone into decline in the later second century AD. The excavations were directed by Andrea Carandini, an experienced archaeologist who at that time had a strong Marxist identity. Settefinestre represented a very important advance in the excavation and publication of Italian rural sites. The dig itself incorporated the best of British field techniques, including the use of student excavators. The final publication was full and meticulous and provided not only a detailed occupation history of the villa, but also information on all categories of the finds from coins to animal bones.

Another important aspect of the project was the research directed toward placing the villa in its immediate landscape and settlement context. Intensive surface surveys were undertaken in the adjoining region of the Ager Cosanus, aiming to document ways in which the rise of the great villa might have contributed to the decline of the small farmers in the area. Some interpretations of the Settefinestre results can be questioned. The subtitle of the final report highlighted Settefinestre's role as a 'villa schiavistica' and made manifest the paradigm of elite social and economic exploitation of slave labour that shaped many interpretations of the excavation.

Marxist paradigms may have been too rigidly applied to the interpretation of Settefinestre's history, and too many generalizations have been made from that single site and its history. Excavations at the nearby elite villa site of Le Colonne showed similarities in occupation history, but also significant differences. However, the overall importance of the Settefinestre project remains. It demonstrated how much can be learned from the careful excavation of a site whose poor surface preservation initially made it seem less than promising. A whole generation of young archaeologists trained at Settefinestre and applied the lessons learned to a range of other projects in Italy and the Roman provinces.

Another major villa excavation demonstrating how much can be learned from careful excavation and interpretation, and providing important insight into the cultural and ideological role of the luxury villa in a very different cultural context, was that at Fishbourne near Chichester near the south coast of England. The remains were discovered by chance in the 1960s, thoroughly excavated and published, and presented as an archaeological tourist site (Cunliffe 1971). The building proved to be an elegant palatial structure of totally Roman design. It was laid out as a courtyard villa with ranges of receiving rooms decorated with mosaics and wall-paintings. The courtyard was graced with formal gardens planted in the Roman manner. This first major palace phase dated to the later first century AD, not long after the Romans first arrived on the island.

Such an early massive complex must have belonged to an important personage, and the palace has plausibly been associated with the family of the Romano-British client king Cogidubnus. Both architecture and garden planting are especially informative about the Romanization of the British elite. The creation of such formal Mediterranean gardens in the very different environment of Britain represented more than just a desire to imitate the lifestyle of the Roman conquerors. As can be seen in colonial America, elites have traditionally used formal gardens as mechanisms of control, employing such displays of rationality and discipline as visual justification for their position of dominance (Leone 1984). The material culture of Fishbourne provided many other insights into the Romanization of the occupants. The dominance of pig bones in the faunal sample showed that they had adopted a characteristic Roman diet with its emphasis on pork consumption.

The villa at Fishbourne was not unique in this Roman client territory of southern England. Similar elegant, early villas have been found nearby. Clearly the Romans were using the villa as a cultural package to encourage the acculturation of their clients.

Even now, in an age of improved archaeological techniques, excavators tend to concentrate on larger villa sites with their long histories, complex architecture and art works associated with upper-class life. Information thus continues to accumulate on an aspect about which we already know a great deal. We long remained much less well informed about Roman rural sites lower down the social and economic scale. This was partly as a result of the lure of the big sites, but it also reflected a peculiar combination of elitist and 'Marxist' views of the countryside. Thus the elitists saw high-status sites as the only really important ones, while the 'Marxists' regarded the domination of the Roman rural world by the plantations and the latifundia as having marginalized and destroyed the world of the smaller farmer. This pattern is beginning to change, and archaeologists have in recent decades begun studying a range of rural residences in different locations and with different histories.

An early (1960s) example of quality excavation and detailed publication of smaller Roman rural sites in the Roman provinces was that of a group of small Roman sites at Shakenoak in North Oxfordshire (Broadribb, Hands & Walker 1971). The sites had a long occupation and provide interesting insight into a part of the Romano-British countryside. The final report, published in a very modest format, was distinguished by its detailed presentation of the full range of evidence recovered, from architecture to faunal material.

A similar pioneering excavation of this type in Italy was conducted in the 1960s at the San Rocco and Posto villas in the Ager Falernus north-west of Capua (Cotton & Metraux 1985).

Careful fieldwork provided data for a detailed reconstruction of the evolution of the villas. That at Posto was small, but the San Rocco villa evolved into a complex of some elegance and sophistication, although nothing on the scale of a Settefinestre. The residential unit received appropriate attention, but the excavators also investigated the *pars rustica*, where elements of a pressing complex were recovered. The researchers also took care to publish the full range of small finds along with the architectural remains in the final report. Their integration of structural history and material culture history was rare for the period and remains rare today for villa excavations. Expressive of the limits of archaeology at that time was the slight attention paid to environmental data.

In the years since the Francolise excavations, a growing number of farmsteads and smaller villas have been investigated using the best current archaeological techniques. They have been of different types with different histories, and have raised different archaeological and historical questions. A good Italian example is the modest, relatively short-lived Republican farmstead of 'Il Giardino' in the territory of Cosa. The complex consisted at its greatest extent of some twenty rooms grouped around a small courtyard. The rooms were mostly small and without ornament. The farm was established in the early second century BC and continued in use until the Augustan period. Its history bridged the period when smaller farms were supposedly being abandoned in the Cosa countryside. It had modest productive facilities, while the presence of coins, amphorae, and commercially produced pottery show that it was tied into the Roman consumer economy. Il Giardino provided a good counterweight to Settefinestre, but again raised the question of how many generalizations can be derived from the study of a single small site.

Indeed, the major problem of villa archaeology lies as much in the scattered and random nature of the sample of thoroughly studied sites as in the uneven nature of our evidence from the older sites. While the number of reasonably well excavated and published villas is increasing, the sample is still small. Moreover, these carefully excavated villas are scattered over the very varied landscape of western Europe and the Mediterranean, with rarely more than one or two illuminating the rural archaeology of a single area.

Other cautionary factors have to be taken into consideration. We know that there were significant differences in the rural development of regions of the Roman Empire. Peregrine Horden and Nicholas Purcell have hammered home that message in their recent book, *The Corrupting Sea* (2000). Moreover, research on rural areas with abundant written as well as physical documentation, such as New England from the seventeenth to the nineteenth century, has demonstrated that farms can fail as much from very local factors such as poor management, bad land, or a succession of poor harvests as from the broader trends that have tended to interest the ancient historian and the classical archaeologist (Cronon 1983).

This combination of local similarity and difference in occupation history can be seen in one of the relatively few clusters of smaller villas that have been excavated and published, that of the villas located near the Roman town of Buccino in Lucania (Dyson 1983). Five Roman rural sites were excavated. Although all the sites were disturbed and all the architectural plans incomplete something of each occupation history could be reconstructed. Each villa had a long history, in some instances stretching from the second century BC to at least the fifth century AD. While they were modest structures by the standards of the great *villae maritimae*, all made some claims to elegance in the form of wall-paintings, baths and mosaics. The finds of glazed pottery, coins and lamps showed strong links into Roman consumer society, while the presence of loom-weights and courtyards with buried storage jars demonstrated an involvement in agricultural and pastoral production. However, each had a different construction and occupation history. The commonality and variety among the Buccino villas shows what can be learned from programmes of multiple villa excavations conducted in a limited area.

The single villa was for a long time the focus of Roman rural archaeology and antiquarian history, and to a certain degree it remains so today. However, with the emergence of ancient history as an academic discipline in the nineteenth century, the concerns of Roman rural studies began to change. Social scientists and historians remained very interested in the Roman countryside, but approached it from a perspective that emphasized social and economic issues related to the structures and historical evolution of rural life. The great German sociologist Max Weber (1858-1917) began his academic career researching the social and economic history of the Roman countryside. Weber was a student of Theodor Mommsen, and as one would expect from a student of Mommsen he approached Roman rural history from a strongly legal perspective. However, he appreciated the value of other source-materials, such as the writings of the *agrimensores* (ancient surveyors), whose technical treatises contained a great deal of little-used information on the development of the Roman countryside (Capogrossi Colognesi 2000). Weber brought to the study of the Roman countryside not only his wide-ranging knowledge of social science, but also his interest in the current problems of rural Germany. His general approach was to stress the economic self-sufficiency of the Roman countryside, and he provided important support for a 'primitivist' vision of Roman rural life that downplayed complex market forces operating in the Roman rural world.

The career of the mature Weber overlapped for a few years with that of the young Michael Rostovtzeff (1870-1952), a Russian historian who was to emerge as the foremost social and economic historian of antiquity in his generation. Rostovtzeff appreciated the importance of the countryside for understanding Roman society, from the complex productivity of the villa to the destructive forces unleashed by the peasantry in the third century AD. He also emphasized that the study of the countryside required the scholar to move beyond the traditional literary and legal texts to the world of inscriptions, papyri and especially art and archaeology. His *Social and Economic History of the Roman World* (1926) with its well-captioned illustrations drawn from archaeology, ranging from Pompeian villa landscape paintings to African mosaics, pioneered the use of material culture to explain ancient historical processes.

Karl Marx and Frederick Engels were far less well informed on ancient rural life than Weber or Rostovtzeff, and in the end far less interested. However, the Roman economy with its 'slave mode of production' based on the plantation estate was regarded by them as an important developmental stage in pre-capitalist economic history. Their interests in Rome as an important pre-capitalist economy influenced communist and Marxist scholars in both the Soviet Union and the West. Special scholarly attention was focused on the Roman rural world of the late second and first centuries BC that produced the aborted attempts at reform of the Gracchi, the rise of the latifundistic plantations and the slave revolts of Sicily and Spartacus.

A major link between the Marxist vision of the Roman countryside and current paradigms of interpretation for Roman rural history has been the scholarship of the British-American Moses Finley (1912-1986). Finley was an American Marxist who fled to England during the McCarthy era and established himself at Cambridge. His Marxism stimulated in him an interest in ancient economic life not found in many classical historians of his generation. Finley stressed the relatively primitive nature of the ancient economies, including that of Rome. His Marxist interests also led him to research ancient slavery, including the plantation-based slavery of Rome. Finley attracted to Cambridge some of the brightest European and American students of his generation. He worked largely with the ancient written sources, although he had a profound knowledge of both economic history and social theory. He was sceptical of the value of archaeology in resolving problems in ancient history, but as a dialectical materialist could not totally reject material culture. A number of his protégés went on to apply archaeology to the problems of Roman rural life.

The fragmentary and chaotic nature of the archaeological evidence for Roman rural life for a long time discouraged historians unfamiliar with material culture from using archaeology in their social and economic interpretations. It was the two pioneering archaeologists of Roman Britain, Francis Haverfield (1860-1919) and Robin Collingwood (1889-1943), who provided some of the first demonstrations of how the generally formless antiquarian literature dealing with the Roman archaeology of rural England could be integrated and used to address important historical questions related to the evolution of the Romano-British countryside. Both scholars worked at the juncture of documentary history and archaeology and appreciated the need to use the material evidence in writing the history of Roman Britain, a province so poorly documented in the written sources.

In the late nineteenth and early twentieth century, when Haverfield and Collingwood were doing their research, the villa was the best known type of site in Britain. It was a distinctly Roman form imported early into the island. While many scholars regarded the villa as an indicator of the settlement of continental Romans in Britain, Haverfield saw its spread as reflecting indigenous Romanization, whereby the native Britons took on the lifestyle of the conqueror. In this, as in other areas in the study of Roman Britain, Haverfield set the agenda for the debate about the nature and extent of Romanization that continues to the present day (Hingley 2000).

As the evidence for the location of villas in Britain was collected and plotted, it became clear that this distinctive Roman rural house form was not evenly distributed throughout the province. The villas were concentrated in the south-east of the island, with relatively few examples documented outside that core zone. Collingwood saw this pattern as an expression of the complementary worlds of Roman villas and native villages, and it became for him the basis of a 'two Britain' vision of the Roman province with the south-east becoming largely Roman and the other areas to the north and west retaining more elements of the pre-Roman Celtic world.

Recent research has forced a rethinking of many of Haverfield's and Collingwood's hypotheses, but they remain important pioneering examples of the use of patterning in the archaeological evidence to answer historical questions. Their research also demonstrated the need to move beyond the villa site and collect evidence on the countryside within a larger archaeological framework. This was to be one of the major developments of the post World War II years.

2

Expanding the Vision:
Survey and a New View of
the Roman Countryside

Renaissance scholars established the practice of exploring and recording standing Roman remains in the countryside, and it has since remained an important activity in Roman archaeology. The Englishman Thomas Ashby (1874-1931) documented many rural sites in the Roman Campagna in the early years of the twentieth century (Hodges 2000). Italian archaeologists such as Lorenzo and Stefania Quilici have continued that topographical survey work, whose urgency has been increased by development and agricultural transformation in the Italian countryside that has led to the destruction of so many archaeological sites. The aims of the Ashby-Quilici type of survey were to record the site remains before they were destroyed, to identify the ruins with places and monuments known to antiquity, and to provide information on sites suitable for excavation. It has been a noble and important archaeological activity, but one whose core aims were antiquarian, topographical and empirical.

In both Europe and the Americas the years immediately after World War II saw the slow and cautious birth of a new approach to survey, one that attempted to bring methods of gathering archaeological data closer to those used in the social sciences. The new approach required improved field methodologies based on more sophisticated research strategies that in the end led to a fuller and better database and allowed the more effective employment of the survey data in the reconstruction of settlement pattern and settlement history. Such research in the Americas was done mostly by anthropological archaeologists and had relatively little impact on classical archaeology (Willey and Sabloff 1980). In the world of British archaeology, where archaeology was considered a more holistic discipline with fewer temporal and geographical divisions, more crossover was possible.

The survey project that was to prove most influential in the creation of a new Roman rural archaeology in the Mediterranean was that undertaken in the Ager Veiantanus after World War II by the British School in Rome (Potter 1979). Its organizer was the new director of the British School, John Ward-Perkins. Ward-Perkins had been a student of Mortimer Wheeler in Britain and brought perspectives learned from British prehistoric and Roman archaeology to the Italian scene. Although Italy was opening up to foreign archaeological projects, the postwar financial problems of the British School precluded major excavations like those of the Americans at Cosa. However, Ward-Perkins saw in the countryside north of Rome that had once belonged to the Etruscan and Roman city of Veii the potential for a long-term survey project that addressed problems of immediate archaeological concern. Agricultural reform and suburban development spreading out from Rome were opening up for exploitation those lands that had been little disturbed since the Roman period. The introduction of mechanical cultivation was revealing hundreds of new archaeological sites, but at the same time rapidly destroying them. It was urgent that these sites be mapped, described, and sampled before they disappeared.

Ward-Perkins began to dispatch students from the British School into the Veii area. They systematically traversed the countryside, identifying and mapping sites of all periods and collecting representative surface-materials, especially ceramics. Three qualities distinguished the Ager Veiantanus surveys from earlier efforts. The research was cumulative, not only increasing the archaeological database, but also allowing the refinement of field methodology through experience and the return to sites for several samplings. The Veii surveyors recorded all sites and not just those with architectural remains and high-status objects visible on the surfaces. They were concerned with all periods from the early prehistoric to the Middle Ages. Materials collected were processed and stored at the British School, providing an ever-expanding and improving database of material culture that could be consulted by archaeologists working not only in the Veii area but throughout Italy.

This expanding body of information provided the basis for a history of the Ager Veiantanus that documented the ebb and flow of settlement from the Etruscan period to the Middle Ages. The surveys around Veii were complemented by similar investigations undertaken in neighbouring areas north of Rome. The settlement history reconstructed from the archaeological material raised serious questions about standard interpretations of such important issues in Roman history as the rise of plantations and the decline of the small farmer in Roman Italy in the later second century BC. However, Roman historians who still felt uncomfortable employing archaeological evidence, especially of the prosaic sort provided by survey, were slow to recognize the importance of this information.

Mediterranean survey archaeology has advanced considerably in research design and field technology since the early days of Veii, and it has become fashionable to criticize Ward-Perkins and his colleagues for their lack of methodological rigour. This is not the place to enter into the debate on survey methodology and the creation of a 'perfect survey'. It should be remembered that the early surveyors of the Ager Veiantanus were working in an empirical British tradition and were not self-conscious New Archaeologists trying to move archaeology toward the 'promised land' of a 'scientific' discipline. Survey archaeologists always work under the limitations posed by each landscape and its history, and flexible empirical approaches may get better results than rigid, abstract field methodologies. The Veii survey produced masses of important information that forced scholars to rethink many aspects of Italian landscape history, stimulated generations of young archaeologists to do survey archaeology, and represents one of the most important contributions ever to the study of the Roman countryside.

One of the most important problems faced by survey archaeologists then and now is that of site definition. For the survey archaeologist the site is usually a surface scatter of varying size and complexity. Some scatters have the full range of artifacts, from architectural elements to quantities of ceramics. Others may produce so few objects that the field worker is hard-pressed to distinguish between the site and the 'background noise' of thin archaeological scatter. Efforts have to be made to bring order and hierarchy to the abundant but ambiguous field data and create a common language for describing sites found during survey. This task is complicated by the fact that each site has a different history, not only of use, but also of post-abandonment transformation by natural and human forces. A site close to the surface that has only recently been disturbed by mechanical ploughing is going to provide information very different from a long exposed one in some abandoned field. Finally, the information yielded by the site is also going to reflect the specific collecting strategy employed by the individual archaeologist.

A standard practice has been to differentiate sites by the extent and composition of the scatter. An extensive scatter at a recently disturbed site should indicate that a large villa lies underneath. This hypothesis would be reinforced by the discovery of fragments of mosaic and wall-painting and large quantities of status pottery. Another scatter, smaller in area and producing only tile, fragments of utilitarian floors, and lesser amounts of glazed pottery, might be identified as a farmstead. Most survey archaeologists feel the need to move beyond vague terms such as 'villa' and establish some system of site hierarchy. Some continue to employ cultural-functional terms such as villa and farmstead, while others prefer more abstract hierarchical classifications based on criteria such as the extent of scatter and the composition of finds. No system can produce a totally accurate settlement picture, given the disjunctions between surface evidence and underground reality. However, most surveys do identify a range of sites and reveal the complex reality of an individual Roman countryside. One of the most important results of survey archaeology has been to make visible the many small farms that once existed in the Roman landscape and force important revisions in our picture of the Roman countryside.

In recent decades survey archaeology in Italy has expanded dramatically, and I can discuss only a limited number of projects here. The Ager Cosanus has been the subject of some of the most intensive survey archaeology in the peninsula. Although American excavations at the Roman town of Cosa started in the late 1940s, at first little interest was shown in the surrounding countryside. By the 1970s, however, the increasing popularity of landscape archaeology and a growing interest in the history of the villa economy of the Ager Cosanus led both American and Italian-British teams to undertake extensive surveys in the colonial hinterland. Some of the same questions that had been raised in the Veii surveys, such as fluctuations in population related to the decline of the small farmer and the rise of large estates in the later Republic, helped shape the Cosa surveys. The field methodologies employed were somewhat different, and data sets produced partly complementary, but in the end the information could be easily integrated. Interpretations of the results, however, varied. The Americans saw similarities between the late Republican Ager Cosanus and Ager Veiantanus and argued that in both cases the decline of the Republican small farmer had been much exaggerated. The Italian-British survey team was part of the Settefinestre excavation project and was more wedded to models that stressed the triumph of the plantation-based slave mode of production. They saw the survey results as supporting their interpretative framework. Such different readings of common archaeological information arose not only from differing ideologies but also from the problem of obtaining from survey material dates of sufficient precision for that material to be used to resolve relatively short-term historical problems.

Other Italian surveys, especially those focused on valley systems, will be considered later. In the rest of continental Europe survey archaeology developed later, although some important work has been undertaken and the future looks very promising. Intensive survey archaeology in the Iberian peninsula is still in its infancy. Jean-Gerard Gorges in his *Les villas hispano-romaines* (1979) has used the published literature to provide a synthetic overview of villa development in the peninsula. Michel Ponsich has used similar material to reconstruct amphora production and villa economy in the Guadalquivir valley. Surveys like that in the Ager Tarragonensis introduced the British model into the area, and now a number of local and regional surveys are producing important information. The southern areas of France lend themselves best to Mediterranean style surveys, and a number of important projects such as those studying micro-regions around Nîmes have yielded good results.

Survey archaeology is beginning to provide a new broad-based vision of the Roman countryside. As a discipline, it has benefited particularly from the new open world of the European Union, where people and ideas travel easily across borders. An impressive number of the projects have been multinational. However, there are discouraging signs that the brief golden age of survey archaeology in Europe may be ending. Development continues to transform the Mediterranean and the continental European landscape at a ferocious rate, destroying large numbers of archaeological sites in the process. At the same time in many areas agricultural activity has contracted, leaving deserted fields where intensive farming once took place. Macchia and woodlands are creeping in, reducing surface visibility and making survey of the Veii type increasingly difficult.

Another region that has seen extensive survey activity is North Africa. Starting in the nineteenth century, the French *Brigade Topographique* began mapping archaeological sites as part of a colonialist strategy that emphasized the connections between Roman and French North Africa. In the countryside the investigators paid special attention to villa ruins with their substantial architectural remains and mosaics. Excavations in the North African hinterland focused on towns and military sites. Aerial photography, while providing documentation for several of the most extensive centuriation grids in the Roman world, also reinforced an historical perspective that stressed this picture of the Roman transformation of rural areas.

The struggle for national independence in North Africa highlighted the contrast between scholars who emphasized the positive contributions of colonialist powers, both ancient and modern, and those who stressed the importance of indigenous cultures and of the resistance against Rome. Archaeology was still dominated by representatives of the colonialist powers, while the alternative vision came more from classical and anthropological research. In some instances the hostilities connected with the struggle for independence brought archaeological activities to a halt. The new nations were in many cases more interested in their Islamic and pre-classical past than in the Roman remains so associated with the ideology of French colonialism.

The Carthage rescue project of the 1970s focused new attention on the archaeological potential of Roman North Africa and especially of Tunisia. An international effort was launched to save significant parts of the site of ancient Carthage from the development associated with the expansion of Tunis. A new generation of archaeologists was introduced to North Africa. The economic history of the Roman Empire was becoming central to the research of more scholars, and the agricultural importance of North Africa for the Roman Empire was increasingly appreciated. The research of John Hays made archaeologists appreciate the importance of African Red Slip pottery both as a dating tool, especially in survey, and as an indicator of the North African export economy. At the same time national and international agencies were funding rural development projects in the area. Both archaeologists and modern development experts were struck by the contrast between the abundant evidence for the intensive development by the Romans of the rural hinterlands of countries such as Tunisia and Libya, and the limited productivity of the same regions today. Archaeological survey work like that of the British in the Libyan countryside attempted to address questions related both to ancient and modern rural development.

Many areas of the North African countryside make ideal survey country. Ground cover is minimal, and there has been limited post-Roman disturbance. The Roman farmsteads were stone-built, and their facilities, such as olive presses, leave sturdy, easily detectable remains. This has proved especially true for Tunisia. Surveys in that country still number less than twenty, but they have studied a variety of zones from the hinterlands of such important coastal centres as Carthage and Lepti Minus to such interior regions as the Kasserine Pass. In all the surveys the archaeologists have been concerned with the types of sites, their occupation histories, and what they tell us about the relations of natives and Romans in the countryside. Hundreds of farmsteads have been mapped and sampled, and we now have an impressive database for Roman rural North Africa that did not exist a few years ago.

The North African farmsteads were often large complexes with impressive stone architecture. Some were relatively open structures designed around courtyards. Others, such as the *gsur*, were enclosed by towered walls. The farmstead at Nador in Morocco, excavated by the Italians, is a good example of such a walled farm whose impressive façade with an inscription naming the owner was designed to impress travellers on the nearby Roman road. However, within that complex all space was devoted to agricultural activity; there was no *pars urbana* characteristic of the true villa. Many of these walled sites had first been identified as forts, but on careful investigation proved to be agricultural facilities. The fortified complexes tend to be later in date and in some areas may reflect growing rural insecurity. However, others, like the farm at Nador, may reflect the desire of the owners to impress their neighbours with monumental architecture.

North African rural sites, like those of other parts of the Roman Empire, varied considerably in size. The rural settlement structure was organized around a complex combination of villages and large and small farmsteads. Bruce Hitchner in his survey in the Cillium-Thelepte region in Tunisia differentiated five settlement types ranging from what he called 'agrovilles', multi-family communities with major olive-pressing facilities, to small farmsteads. The Sufetula-Masclianae survey, conducted in an area 30 kilometres south-west of the Roman city of Cillium in Tunisia, documented nine farms with a scatter measuring more than 5 hectares, twenty-one with 1-5 hectares, and ninety-five smaller than 1 hectare. In the Sidi el-Hani survey area, three-quarters of the 104 sites mapped were less than 0.5 hectares. In the Carthage survey thirteen villas, fifty-five small farmsteads and eleven villages were identified.

The olive press has become one of the most important economic indicators of the North African surveys. Both the pressing floors and the stone uprights for the presses themselves are well preserved and easily identifiable. They are key documents for one of the most massive of Roman export industries – North African olive oil. North Africa was famous for its grain productivity during the Roman period, and it became a major supplier for the city of Rome. However, grain production cannot be documented easily by archaeological survey. By contrast, the production centres for olive oil can be identified through the press complexes. Each press probably serviced some 500-1,000 mature olive trees, well beyond the needs of any individual household (Hitchner 1989: 400). It seems probable that North African farmers did not invest in a press unless they were into the export business. However, large numbers have been documented in the North African countryside. In one Tunisian survey, thirty-one out of seventy rural sites had presses. In another there were twenty-nine oil complexes for forty-three farms. David Mattingly has estimated that 1,500 km^2 of land in Libya supported 350 olive oil presses.

Most farmsteads with olive pressing facilities started in the late Republic and the early Empire. However, many, like Nador, continued to be occupied into the Vandalic period of the fifth century. Indeed, the evidence from the rural finds of transport amphorae suggest that productivity may actually have increased. The ethnic origins of the farmers engaged in these activities in most cases cannot be determined, and probably after a certain historical point became irrelevant. French colonialist scholars have stressed the impact of new Roman settlement. The farmers were seen as Roman colonists who, like their French *pied noir* successors, made the land productive. Certainly the role of Roman colonization in the development of the North African countryside cannot be ignored. From the late second century BC onward we have references to Roman settlers arriving in North Africa. The extensive Roman centuriation grids provide further proof of the Roman determination to import farmers. However, much of the survey research has taken place in areas like the hinterlands of Carthage that were massively transformed by Rome, and even now relatively little has been undertaken in the territories of the pre-Roman/early-Roman indigenous states such as Numidia. Research in rural areas of interior Libya that were definitely not settled by Rome show the natives making some of the same transformations into the agrarian market economy.

The emphasis in most surveys has been on settlements and residential units. They have demonstrated that most of the Roman countryside supported diverse settlement types. While survey archaeology does not allow us to reconstruct precise social and economic structures, some generalizations can be made from that evidence. Slave-based villas certainly existed in large numbers, but the chain-gang did not dominate the Roman countryside. Both a free peasantry and tenant farmers must have been common in many areas. Clearly much of the Roman countryside was tied into a market economy, with all the positives and negatives that entailed.

This new research has also made clear that the student of the Roman rural economy needs to consider more than just farming. Archaeology is providing important information on other types of rural production. We have a growing appreciation of the complex role of manufacturing and extractive activities as well as other forms of rural exploitation, from pastoral activities to marine and forest production. All this further undermines the view of the Roman rural world as a relatively simple and rather autarkic place with a highly stratified society and limited involvement with the wider Roman world. Two areas where new archaeological information has been especially important in restructuring our thinking have been ceramic production and mining.

The Roman ceramic industry (and the term 'industry' is used here advisedly) was the most complicated that had existed before the development of the British Midlands potteries by such eighteenth-century entrepreneurs as Josiah Wedgwood. Most ceramic production took place in the countryside or around rural small towns where supplies of clay and firewood were plentiful. Manufacturing sites with their sturdy kilns and broad scatters of potsherds and wasters are easily identified through field survey, or the combination of survey and various forms of geophysical investigation. Three large but different ceramic industries set in rural environments were the amphora industry, the mass-marketed red wares known as *terra sigillata*, and the specialized local and regional ceramic wares used mainly for cooking and eating. Some highlight the importance of long-distance trade for the development of the Roman countryside, but others show the complexity and diversity of the local and regional markets that brought the benefits of the consumer society to a range of rural Romans.

In the Roman Empire the amphora was the fundamental vessel used for the transport of liquids in bulk. Amphorae have been found in enormous quantities at both land and underwater sites. Distinctive characteristics of form and materials allow them to be dated and provenanced with considerable precision. Since the vessels were large and heavy, it was practical to manufacture them close to the places where they were first to be used, and this often meant production in rural areas, for the amphorae were mainly used for the shipping of agricultural produce, especially wine and olive oil. Rural amphorae kiln sites have been identified in increasing numbers in those Mediterranean areas that were major players in the agricultural export market. Kilns for amphora production in Italy have been found close to centres of wine production. Such kilns were also often general pottery production centres turning out bricks, tiles and other items for rural use (Peacock 1977). The research of Michel Ponsich in the Guadalquivir valley in southern Spain (the Baetis valley in the Roman provice of Baetica) has located many kiln sites and demonstrated the complex symbiotic relationship between amphora manufacture and the production and marketing of olive oil from the southern Iberian peninsula.

The amphora is an archaeological artifact that can be traced from the source of its shipment to the place of its destruction. They are found in great numbers in underwater wrecks and are also abundant at 'consumption' sites, including spectacular dumps such as Monte Testaccio in Rome. Students of the amphora trade have used amphora information to map shifts in the trade in wine and olive oil, both to Rome and to other areas of the Empire. This trade information has in turn been related to cycles of prosperity and depression in different areas of the Roman countryside. The widespread export of wines from the Ager Cosanus by families such as the Sestii during the early first century BC helped to create the fortunes that made possible the construction of elegant villas such as Settefinestre and Le Colonne. The replacement of Italian wine on the Roman market by that produced in other areas probably contributed to the decline of the great Cosa estates. Markets in olive oil showed similar instability. A major shift occurred in the third century AD when Baetica was replaced by North Africa as a major source of olive oil for the city of Rome.

The economic insights provided by amphorae are important, but again they have to be applied with caution. The dating of amphorae such as those from the Baetis valley has been steadily refined, and the new dates suggest that the export of Baetican oil continued into the fourth century, although certainly at a reduced level compared with earlier centuries. Moreover, many sites in the Baetis valley continued to be occupied into the fourth century AD, if not later (Jones 1988). This is a good example of the danger of reading Roman rural economic history with a paradigm too focused on large estates. The decline of olive oil exports certainly had its impact on regional prosperity, but it did not lead to the abandonment of all Baetican rural establishments. Most had presumably always practised a mixed economy, so that the decline of the olive oil market meant a loss in prosperity but not utter catastrophe.

More complicated were the dynamics of the great glazed ceramics centres. During the first century BC, potters around the town of Arretium (modern Arezzo) in central Italy turned the production of red-glazed moulded ceramics into a mass industry. The town of Arretium where the actual production was located was a small and relatively isolated place. Presumably it was the combination of clay and timber in the surrounding countryside that drew the potters there. Stamps with personal and business names impressed on the pots have allowed the reconstruction of an economic sociology of this industry which at its height represented the most massive output of pottery that Europe would see before the eighteenth century (Peacock 1982).

As new large markets for fancy ceramics developed in Gaul, in the Rhine garrison areas and ultimately in Britain, the potters moved north, bringing their moulds with them and seeking out places with clay and wood resources in the new territories. Major new centres for status ceramic production were established at sites such as La Graufesenque and Lezoux, in south and central France respectively. These were again massive operations turning out tens of thousands of vessels and generating substantial income for those who owned and managed the workshops. They had large, complex workforces of free, freed, and slave workers. Most were located in rural areas, often at a considerable distance from major centres. Some operated for centuries. They created a major cash-driven export business connecting these rural production centres to many parts of the Roman Empire. Most research has focused on the social, economic and technical organization of the workshops themselves and the distribution patterns of their wares. Less has been done on their impact on the surrounding catchment areas. However, like military centres, these potteries need to be supplied with food, goods and services. Their long-term presence must have shaped their rural hinterlands in distinctive ways.

Rather different were the organization and impact of the local and regional ceramic industries. Only recently have archaeologists paid serious attention to the non-status pottery of the Roman Empire. These 'table' and 'kitchen' wares were produced in a variety of fabrics and forms reflecting complex culinary activities during the Roman period. They were almost never made by household potters, but produced at medium-large manufacturing centres serving specific regional market areas. The archaeologists of Roman Britain have identified a

49

number of these specialized ceramic producers in places like the Nene valley and have reconstructed the distribution pattern of their wares. One such ceramic production centre operated at Water Newton near Peterborough. A Roman community was located nearby, and both the local river and a major Roman road facilitated shipment to regional markets. The developer of the ceramic industry may well have been the wealthy landowner whose villa was located near the pottery.

Many kilns have been discovered near villa sites. Some served clearly household needs by producing items such as tiles and amphorae. Others manufactured for the regional market, turning out utilitarian pottery as well as lamps and the clay figurines so important for dedications at local religious shrines. Villa production was certainly complemented by that of craftsmen located in the *vici* (small towns). What is always striking is the variety of the products. A recent study of a rural lamp production centre in France showed how one manufacturer copied shapes and decorations directly from outside models and then supplied a variety of those imitations to the local market.

The economic implications of such ceramic markets are very important for an understanding of the complexity of the rural system. Most of these items had to be purchased. Their presence at a small rural site means that the inhabitants of even a humble settlement had sold enough surplus to purchase such items at the local market. The variety of forms suggests an impressive range of household activities. A comparison of the pottery found at a Roman-British farmstead with that from its medieval equivalent demonstrates clearly how much more complex was Roman ceramic usage.

Another important Roman rural industry was mining. The mines tended to be located in rural areas. Under the Roman Republic mining was more often the domain of community entrepreneurs or private associations, while under the Empire the mining of precious metals was increasingly under imperial control. The mining enterprise involved not only the extraction of ore, but also the preliminary processing that turned the ore into more transportable metal pigs. It has generally been regarded as one of the most brutal of Roman operations, a world of soldiers, slaves and criminals that would have been largely self-contained and therefore would have had limited impact on the rural areas where the mines were located. In certain instances that was true, but a totally autarkic mining operation was not feasible. Large numbers of people worked at the mines: Strabo mentions that 40,000 were employed at the mines near Carthago Nova. The personnel administering the mines required supplies, especially foodstuffs, timber and iron tools, and these had to be provided by the adjoining rural areas. Some could be requisitioned, but others had to be purchased on the open market.

Recent Spanish research has provided insight into the complex rural world that developed around two mining centres (Orejas & Sanchez-Palencia 2002). The first was the later republican/early imperial silver and lead mines near Carthago Nova. Survey has revealed a large number of sites in the areas of the mine. Some provided direct labour and services to the mines, while others engaged in regular agricultural and fish-processing activities that certainly benefited from the presence of the 'mine markets'. The local elites appear to have controlled the mines and to have benefited from their exploitation. In contrast, the gold mines of the north-west Iberian peninsula developed as more tightly controlled imperial operations. However, indigenous communities provided at least some of the labour, and a complex network of indigenous, Romanized and Roman settlements developed in the areas around the mines.

The production of gold, silver, and other precious metals was increasingly controlled by the central government. That was clearly not the case with minerals such as iron, which was required for a great range of rural activities. The inhabitants of the countryside therefore needed to develop as many iron mines as possible. The ore was smelted and utensils forged near where it was extracted. Recent fieldwork in rural France has produced evidence for many such Roman mining and forging operations, most of them small and short-lived. In the Franche Comté area sixty iron-working sites were mapped, mainly located near small village settlements rather than villas. The same was true of the forty-five iron production centres in the Maconnais (Leroy *et al.* 2000). Those were clearly cases of local production for locals.

However, this was not always the case. In Britain, the Roman iron-mining operations in the Weald area of south-east England reached a scale that was not to be seen again until the Industrial Revolution of the late eighteenth century (Dark & Dark 1997) . In France, the archaeologists studying the iron-mining site of Grand Ferrier des Forges near Martyres (Aude) estimated that 37,000 tons of iron were produced there between the middle of the first century BC and the mid-third century AD. Graffiti at the site show that Latin speakers as well as natives were involved in production operations. It has been estimated that some 100 miners and their families were resident there, suggesting a community rather than a slave barracks (Decombeix *et al.* 2000).

Farmers, potters, miners and all other inhabitants of the countryside depended on the political, social, economic and religious services that local communities provided. Almost all of the rural areas studied here were articulated around 'official' communities bearing various names such as *colonia*, *municipia* and *civitas*. While considerable research has been done on the internal history and archaeology of such centres, much less has been done to investigate the symbiotic relationships between town and country. At Cosa in Etruria, extensive research has been conducted on both town and country, but until very recently little was done to integrate the archaeological evidence from the two worlds and show how they operated within a single system. The work of Philippe Leveau at Caesarea in Mauretania represents one of the best integrated studies of a

Roman community and its territory that we have, although important town-country research is being conducted at other places, such as Tarragona in Spain.

The life of the countryside was also shaped by a range of other, smaller communities with ancient names such as *fora* and *vici* and modern designations such as 'small towns' (Burnham & Wacher 1990). While most of those centres had no official status, they played a variety of social, economic and religious roles in rural life. In Gaul 192 *vici* have been identified, and 54 'small towns' in Roman Britain. Such places are well attested in all areas of the Roman West. Some developed as road stations and others as religious centres and health spas. Their main functions were as service and production centres for the surrounding countryside. Those located on major roads provided links between local producers and the wider Roman economy. The periodic markets that are well documented in the literary and epigraphic record, but hard to document archaeologically, took place there (De Light 1993). Such a centre was Aquae Siccae (modern St Cizy in the Haute Garonne) located on a major Toulouse-Pyrenees road. The site, which spread over some eight hectares, was occupied from the High Empire into the early fifth century AD. The presence of kilns shows ceramic production, while the large number of loom-weights suggests weaving workshops that consumed the wool from the local flocks.

Survey archaeology since World War II has revolutionized the way we look at the Roman countryside. Our data pool on Roman rural sites has increased massively, and this has allowed the student of Roman history to move beyond the literary and epigraphical sources and the villa-oriented archaeology of the antiquarian tradition. This new information has made it clear that the Roman countryside was far more complex and diverse socially, economically and demographically than previously suspected. Because of the quantity, the specialized nature, and at times the inaccessibility of this new archaeological data, as well as strong reluctance to abandon older, more simplistic models of rural development, many Roman historians and even Roman archaeologists have not used it to the degree that it deserves.

Earlier survey research certainly had its limitation. Most of the pioneering surveys were focused on the documentation of Roman sites and the reconstruction of Roman settlement history. The dominance of paradigms of colonial-style Romanization in ancient historiography certainly led to the under-representation of indigenous survivals and alternative systems of rural social and economic organization. While the survey pioneers, especially those from Britain and France, were often very sensitive to landscape history, they did not always work with specialists such as geographers and geologists and did not have the information supplied by techniques such as GIS (geographic information system) or, in the early days, even systematic aerial photography. The movement from a settlement archaeology to a true landscape archaeology that has shaped more recent research will be the subject of the next chapter.

3

Aerial Photography, Landscape Archaeology and a Macrovision of the Roman Countryside

The application of aerial photography to archaeology began in the period between the World Wars. Pioneers in England, such as the archaeologist O.G.S. Crawford and Major G.W.G. Allen, discovered that buried building remains created differential crop growth and that this resulted in light and dark patterns that could be detected on aerial photographs. Structures and features that were not identifiable on the ground became clearly visible in photographs taken from the air. While the new technique could and did make important contributions to our understanding of the development of classical and medieval cities, its major potential lay in the study of rural areas. In their flights over the English countryside, the photographers documented a whole range of new sites. Especially prominent were Roman military camps and Roman villas.

In the same period the Frenchman, Père Antoine Poidebard, was demonstrating the worth of aerial photography for discovering sites in the arid and semi-arid desert and pre-desert. Shadow-effects produced by sand building up against standing walls proved as useful for detecting sites as crop marks. That tradition of aerial research was continued by Colonel Jean Baradez in Algeria, and his 1949 book *Fossatum Africae* showed the quantities of information that aerial photography could provide on sections of the Roman landscape that were difficult to access on the ground.

World War II gave a whole new impetus to the application of aerial photography to archaeology. Techniques were refined and equipment improved, and much of Europe and the Mediterranean was extensively documented by reconnaissance flights during the war. Afterwards, a group of far-sighted scholars, led by John Ward-Perkins of the British School at Rome, arranged for the preservation of these military photographs in archaeological research centres. The English archaeologist John Bradford soon demonstrated their worth in reconstructing the long history of rural Italy from the Neolithic enclosures to the Roman land divisions (Bradford 1957).

The World War II photographs proved tremendously useful, but they had their limitations. Most were high-altitude images, good for detecting larger patterns such as Roman land divisions, but less effective in providing information on individual sites. The time and place of the photography reflected the demands of the military. The archaeologists working on individual sites and even clusters of sites needed images shot at lower altitudes. The season of the year and the time of day when the photograph was taken proved crucial in revealing the maximum archaeological information. Specialists such as Kenneth St Joseph of Cambridge began organizing systematic campaigns of archaeological air photography. Through the 1950s, 1960s and 1970s, and down to the present day, the inventory of Roman rural sites detected through aerial photography has increased massively. The results have been especially impressive in England and parts of France, where crop conditions and the structures of the countryside make archaeological air photography especially effective.

The overall aerial photographic record of the Roman countryside that we have today is a very uneven one, reflecting not only the ground conditions in specific areas and the interests of archaeologists, but also political and military sensitivities. Britain and France have been extensively covered. So has former French North Africa. For Italy the picture is uneven. The Iberian peninsula had one of the oldest, richest, and most complicated Roman landscapes with a number of different periods of colonization and land reorganization. However, the area has seen little in the way of aerial photographic research. In spite of the fact that it has provided one of the rare examples of a bronze cadastral map, Iberia has yielded few undisputed examples of centuriation grids (Jones 2000).

Aerial photography works best with certain types of sites. Villas, especially major villas with masonry walls and extensive areas of mosaic, tile and cement floors, are easily identified. Archaeologists who have long based their reconstructions of elite Roman rural development on a limited number of villas, often poorly excavated, now have a rapidly expanding sample of new sites. Since aerial photographs can provide information on the overall organization not only of the central villa units, but of the outbuildings as well, they have improved the archaeologist's ability to formulate structural typologies and create historical syntheses of villa development. The photographs rovide precise locational information enabling the sites to be easily positioned and visited. They provide the basis for an efficient programme of surface samplings and soundings that allow a range of sites to be dated.

One of the most important programmes of regional aerial photography has been that conducted by Roger Agache in the Somme region of north-eastern France (Agache 1978). The open countryside of Picardy, with its expanses of grain fields, provided ideal conditions for aerial archaeological detection. Regular overflights revealed large numbers of villas, shrines and other Roman rural sites. Agache, in his final publication of the survey, discussed over a hundred villa sites alone. While few could be extensively excavated, the French archaeologists were able to combine aerial photographic and limited excavation data to reconstruct the Roman rural history of the area.

The prosperity of the Roman countryside of the Somme region derived in part from the fertile soil that still makes the area one of the breadbaskets of France. It was also a product of wider political and strategic developments. This rapid expansion of the Somme villa economy during the early Empire was stimulated by the need to supply the garrisons on the Rhine and the service communities that surrounded them. It serves as a corrective to the view that the presence of the Roman army was merely extractive and oppressive and could not be a force for real growth. The Roman military could requisition many of their supplies, but clearly that did not meet all needs. The large, well-paid communities of soldiers and their dependants were bound to create massive market possibilities that the Somme landowners exploited.

One important application of aerial photographic research that has been closely related to colonialist interpretations of Roman rural development has been the study of centuriation systems. The Romans were not the first to employ systematic programmes of rural land division. Aerial photography has revealed extensive evidence for regular land divisions around Greek colonies in various parts of the Mediterranean. However, the Romans applied it most extensively, and by the transformative quality of their centuration programmes made them almost a metaphor for their domination. Indicative of the importance that the Romans attached to formal organizations of newly acquired landscapes is the abundant surviving literature attributed to the *gromatores* or land surveyors. Earlier scholars such as Max Weber used that information effectively. However, before aerial photography archaeologists were hard-pressed to document the activities of these *gromatores* on the ground. A certain number of boundary stones, including some dating back to the period of the Gracchan land reforms of the late second century BC, had been discovered. Occasionally, small traces of Roman land divisions were reconstructed from small-scale topographic maps. However, most activities of the *gromatores* remained invisible. This changed when the high-altitude photographs from World War II were made available to archaeologists.

John Bradford early appreciated the information such photographs could provide on centuriation in areas of intense Roman settlement such as the Po valley. Such early investigations have now been expanded by the research of British and Italian scholars on centuriation grids and colonization along the Via Aemilia in northern Italy. Ferdinando Castagnoli conducted pioneering research on centuriation grids in places like Cosa. However, it has been the French, with a tradition of cadastral land divisions going back to Napoleonic times, who have developed the field of centuriation research most effectively.

Early French investigations centred on North Africa, where they reconstructed a complex centuriated landscape that extended for thousands of kilometres through what are now Algeria, Tunisia and Libya. This emphasis on documenting the Roman transformation of the indigenous landscape was not without its political agenda. French archaeology in North Africa had long had as one of its aims the creation of links between Roman and French colonialism. The research on centuriation came at an especially sensitive time, when the French hold on North Africa was threatened by increasingly powerful national independence movements. The new archaeological information allowed them to highlight the benefits that colonial rule could bring to an underdeveloped rural world.

French archaeologists have not limited their centuriation studies to North Africa. Special attention has been paid to southern Italy, where aerial photography has provided information not only on early Roman land division projects, but also on the ways in which the earlier Greek colonists had made their mark on the land. Provence has provided much evidence. That research received further stimulus from the discovery in 1949 at Orange of fragments of a stone-carved cadastral map dating to the period of Vespasian. It documented three different grid systems and provided the basis for integrated epigraphical and aerial photographic research.

The new information on Roman centuriation demonstrates the historical complexity of the phenomenon. The land divisions revealed by aerial photographs differ markedly in the size and shape of individual plots and in the orientation of specific grids. Clearly they mirror the long history of Roman land divisions from the colonies of the middle Republic, to the late second-century BC Gracchan reforms, to the multiple allocations of land to military veterans during the late Republic and Empire. Associating specific centuriation grids with specific historical events has proven to be extremely difficult, for the surveying process itself left little datable archaeological evidence. Sometimes grids can be related to a major road whose initial construction can be dated, and that can provide a *terminus ante quem* chronological fix for a particular grid.

The emphasis on centuriation and the Roman-shaped countryside that it reveals has contributed to a neglect of other Roman-period field-systems that reflect continuities with the pre-Roman past and the survival of indigenous patterns of land-use during the Roman period. The problem is a complicated one. The European countryside is a palimpsest of field layouts reflecting every period from the Neolithic to the present. Even regular divisions that appear Roman in date may turn out to be the products of much later land reforms. However, if we are to evaluate the Roman landscape, we have to have a clearer idea of what survived from the past into the Roman period, as well as what the Romans created anew. Archaeologists using a combination of material found in and around the fields and the relation of certain field-patterns to known pre-Roman and Roman sites have been able to assign certain examples of more traditional land-divisions to the Roman period. When we turn from the study of the centuriated to the non-centuriated what becomes most striking is the large percentage of land in both Italy and the provinces that was never touched by the *agrimensores*. This is a strong argument for rural continuities from the pre-Roman past, to which we shall return.

Research on Roman roads has a long-standing ambivalent relationship to the study of the countryside. Certainly nothing is more striking in many an aerial photograph than the straight line of a Roman road striding across the land. The only comparable markers until very recently were railway tracks. Like the railway in the nineteenth century the Roman trunk roads transformed rural areas in Europe by providing new access to the larger world. However, Roman historians have stressed the strategic aspects of road-building and have been reluctant to think of the Roman roads in such local terms.

Other factors help to explain the limited interest in the local impact of the Roman road system. One is economic. Roman historians have been much influenced by the discussions of Richard Duncan-Jones on the prohibitively high cost of land transport in the Roman world. If land transport was so expensive it could not have played a major role in rural economic development. Such arguments have reinforced the position of the 'primitivists' who stressed the autarkic isolation and simple, stratified structures of Roman country life.

The whole issue of land transport needs rethinking. Students of the Roman road system, such as Ray Laurence (1999), are now arguing that the deterrent impact of land transport costs has been exaggerated. Certainly archaeology provides abundant evidence for the circulation of large quantities of imported consumer goods in rural areas well removed from usable waterways. Many important Roman export enterprises such as potteries were not located close to good water transport. Such shippers had no choice but to use the roads. North Africa provides especially good examples of this. Unlike Gaul, Spain, or even Britain, North Africa did not have many waterways suitable for year-round transport. Despite this, interior North

Africa became one of the greatest producers of such bulky agricultural commodities as olive oil. Much of the enormous African production of olive oil had to be brought down to the seaports by road. Even in Spain where there were major waterways, these did not always provide immediate access to the actual production areas. In the Guadalquivir valley, olive oil had to be transported first from the upland farms by road and then 'repackaged' in amphorae to be shipped by river and sea to Rome. The ceramic industry provides comparable examples. By no means all of the great pottery production centres had direct easy access to major waterways. Thousands of fragile vessels made much of their long passage from kiln to consumer along roads.

Emphasis on the study of the great trunk roads with their pavings, their milestones and their way-stations carefully documented in the itineraries, has led to the neglect of the study the secondary and tertiary roads that in capillary fashion fed the main system, facilitating regional and local communication. In part this has been the result of deficiencies in documentation, both epigraphical and archaeological. Those smaller roads did not have milestones and their more simple construction materials have not survived. The neglect of the totality of the road system is also partly the result of scepticism concerning the economic complexity of the Roman countryside. A multi-level road system implied a sophistication of rural exchange that many 'primitivists' were unwilling to accept. However, careful studies of local road developments in areas such as south-east England have revealed complicated road systems with some parts built by the state, some by local governments, and some by individual local landowners (Rivet 1969: 178, fig. 5.1). In certain areas pre-Roman trackways remained in use.

The Roman countryside was more than just villas, roads and field systems. The application of older techniques such as survey and aerial photography and newer instruments such as satellite photography and GIS analysis to the ancient landscape have increasingly forced archaeologists and ancient historians to approach the Roman landscape in more holistic terms, considering not only the full range of settlement evidence, but also the interconnections between man-made and natural processes. Rural research increasingly involves not only surveyor, excavator and artifact specialist, but also geographer, geologist and biologist, each providing a special insight into how the Romans shaped their rural world.

The study of river valley systems in the Mediterranean has become a particular focus for this type of more holistic archaeology. In the new world of archaeology that developed after World War II, river valleys in both the Americas and the Mediterranean increasingly attracted researchers. Particularly in marginal environments, river valleys focus human activities and concentrate habitation. They become important communication and transport routes and can provide information on human settlement over long periods of time. Since river valleys are shaped by complex human and natural processes, they can become interesting laboratories for the geologist and the environmental archaeologist.

The Biferno river valley project in east central Italy well illustrates this type of valley-oriented interdisciplinary field research. The director, Graeme Barker, is a prehistoric archaeologist whose research orientation was shaped both by the surveys of the South Etruria project and by the environmental archaeology developed at Cambridge University by Eric Higgs. The valley he selected linked the mountainous areas of the Apennines with the Adriatic coast. Because of its soil and water resources and its access to a variety of environmental zones, the Biferno valley had a long history of settlement. At the same time the valley was well removed from Rome and the major communication networks of Roman Italy. The archaeologists could study a 'longue durée' settlement history that had not been overly distorted by close connection with the imperial power.

One aspect of the Biferno countryside that especially interested Barker and his team was the historical role of pastoralism in shaping its rural economy and society. The valley had until recent times been an important transhumance route, connecting upland summer and lowland winter pastures. The researchers sought to project the early modern history of Biferno valley pastoralism back into the Roman and pre-Roman periods and relate it to larger issues of animal husbandry in the economy of ancient Rome. Evaluating the historical importance of the pastoral economy is never easy (Biddick 1989), for pastoralism is by its very nature a mobile activity and does not leave much in the way of physical remains. French archaeologists have recovered evidence for Roman sheepfolds in the upland La Crau near Arles in southern France, a region where the arrival of veteran settlers from the Samnite and Umbrian regions of Italy may have stimulated transhumant activities (Conges 1997). Fortunately the shepherds of that area were tied into the Roman market economy and left behind enough pottery and coins to allow their sites to be dated. Those artifacts showed that the sheepfolds remained in use from the first century BC to the fifth century AD, demonstrating the long history of pastoral activities in that region. However, such physical evidence for the world of the shepherds is rare (Baden, Brun & Conges 1996). Pastoral-related activities such as weaving and cloth production leave behind few major structures. Small spinning- and weaving-related artifacts such as spindle-whorls and loom-weights can provide evidence for cloth production at a particular site. The presence of numbers of loom-weights and stamped spindle-whorls at S. Pietro-Tolve in Lucania show that the owners of the villa were involved in cloth production, while their absence from the equally well excavated site of Ruoti also in Lucania suggests that that villa played a different role in the pastoral economy. However, such humble objects are poorly documented at many sites and the information they provide on pastoral production is under-represented.

The Biferno archaeologists were sensitive to the complexity of animal-crop relations and reconstructed a Roman rural world in which pastoralism and agriculture were balanced in a complex rural survival strategy rather than in perpetual conflict. The presence at one Roman farmstead of pig bones roughly equal to those of sheep shows an emphasis on household meat as well as wool production.

Discussions of the relative importance of agricultural and pastoral activities need to be informed by sophisticated analyses of faunal assemblages. Since scholars have too long thought that all the information they needed about Roman animal husbandry could be obtained from the literary sources, faunal studies from Roman rural sites for far too long remained rare. The sample of well studied sites in Italy is still very small and that from most of the western provinces is not much better. Roman Britain is much better represented, but here as in other aspects of the study of the Roman countryside, the danger exists that the high quality British research information will skew our overall view of the use of animal resources in the Roman Empire.

However, an increasing number of good faunal studies is being published, and a fuller picture of the production and consumption of meat in the countryside is beginning to emerge. The most detailed and sophisticated publication of faunal material from a Roman site in Italy is that of the animal bone material from the late imperial villa at San Giovanni di Ruoti in Lucania. At Ruoti the richest deposits dated from the fifth/sixth century AD, and are dominated by pig bones.

This reinforces other studies on the importance of pig meat in the Roman diet. Italy has never been good cattle country. However, sheep are omnipresent, and one would expect them to dominate the Roman faunal samples. That is not the case, however. We know that by the late third century AD the city of Rome was consuming vast amounts of pork. By the early fourth century large numbers of pigs were being driven from South

Italy to the capital. However, this centrality of pork consumption starts earlier. Pig bones are dominant in archaeological deposits of the late Republic. The villa at Settefinestre had a piggery on the premises, and the animal bone samples from both Settefinestre and Le Colonne yield a high percentage of pig.

The enthusiasm for pork seems to have been a distinctly Romano-Italic culture trait, and it is worthwhile to compare the Italian results with those of other provinces (King 1999). Of special interest is how the Roman faunal profiles from various provinces compared with those of the pre-Roman period and what that says about the impact of the Roman conquest on diet. In Spain cattle had played an important part in pre-Roman dining rituals. The eating of pork increased under the Roman occupation, but beef consumption also remained strong. In Libya sheep/goat were the dominant meats throughout both the pre-Roman and Roman eras with little change over time. In Gaul pig bones are frequently dominant at town sites, especially in the south, again an expression of the dietary Romanization that one expects to find in the oldest Gallic province. Beef remained more popular in northern Gaul. At Iron Age sites in Britain sheep bones are most common. However, by the late Roman period cattle and pig came to dominate the faunal samples at the more acculturated sites. However, sheep consumption remained strong in the non-villa areas.

Animal production and consumption were economic sectors where the demands of the military must have impacted rural life. The military diet favoured beef, and the military had a great need for other bovine products such as hides. This was reflected in the economy of an area such as Batavia in the Netherlands, where villas are rare and the faunal samples demonstrate the continued importance of cattle. Cattle-raising may also have been a feature of the distinctly non-Roman rural landscape north of Hadrian's wall.

The Romans were not content simply to measure the land

and distribute it to new settlers. They strove to enhance its productivity. In some cases this involved the drainage of marshy or swampy land. In others it meant the development of irrigation schemes to bring arid land into cultivation. Recent archaeological work has done much to help us understand both these processes.

Research on the conversion of fenlands, swamp and marshland to farming has centred on northern Europe, especially England. Fenland research in eastern England has a long history. Two key questions have been the extent of the systematic drainage and the degree to which the Roman civilian or military authorities were involved in such improvements. Most recently Timothy Potter of the British Museum and his colleagues undertook a long-range interdisciplinary study of changes in the Fenland areas east of Cambridge during the Roman period. The research documented major Roman land reclamation schemes that Potter thought must have been the result of imperial intervention. He placed special emphasis on the second/third-century Fenland island settlement of Stonea, dominated by a towered structure that served as a market centre and also as a focus of Romanization.

Potter was not the first to argue that the Fenland reclamations had to have had imperial support. Ian Richmond thought the area might have been a special military district. The approach that stresses imperial intervention has not convinced all Fenland experts, which is not surprising at this moment, when the role of the indigenous populations in shaping Roman Britain is receiving more attention. There is now more evidence for a well established Iron Age society exploiting a mixture of agricultural, pastoral and natural resources in parts of the Fens that continued into the Roman period. Minimalists would acknowledge that the Romans did open up new areas for settlement, but would argue that settlements expansion owed as much to opportunistic exploitation of sea-level changes as to large land-reclamation projects. Even the new settlers seem to have been Romanized natives. In general their settlements remained poor, with the villas mainly established in the areas bordering on the Fens (Fincham 1999).

The evidence for the fenland settlements in Cambridgeshire has now been complemented by information on other projects in different parts of England. Again we can see a balance of public and private initiatives. Some 350 hectares of tidal wetland downstream from Gloucester were reclaimed under the Romans. Some of the schemes are so extensive that they must have been undertaken by the military. Others were more limited and seem to represent private initiatives. Evidence is emerging for similar land development schemes in other countries. Aerial photographs of land along the Po River near Verona provide evidence for Roman divisions that seem related to the drainage and cultivation of marginal lands (Tozzi & Harari 1984). Similar efforts have been documented at Suessa Aurunca north of Naples.

Students of the landscape both ancient and modern have tended to denigrate the worth of 'marginal' areas like coastal marshlands and underestimate the importance of their resources for a rural population (Traina 1988). All societies involved in stock-raising need salt. Recently much more attention has been paid to the role of salt production in coastal areas. Implements used in salt production can be identified archaeologically, allowing the location of salterns to be identified. They have now been found in considerable numbers in many diverse areas of the Roman Empire, from the Mediterranean to the coast of Britain. In some areas the salterns served pastoral needs, while in others salt was used in the fish-processing industry.

The transformation of dry zones into productive farmland during the Roman Empire has also been the object of much new archaeological research. Extensive systems of water control have been identified in North Africa, as well as in other parts of the Roman Empire such as Spain and Portugal. Scholars have long debated whether the Romans expanded agricultural activity through the development of major water control schemes or whether the evidence for Roman farming in now deserted or underutilized lands reflects the impact of climate change or centuries of overgrazing and destructive agricultural practices. Colonialist attitudes to indigenous peoples and their inefficient use of land have played a shaping role in the debate. Important for the resolution of this question has been the UNESCO British research in Libya. One area that the archaeologists focused on was the Tripolitanian pre-desert (Gilbertson, Hunt & Gillmore 2000). Today the region is only marginally farmed, but the British discovered some 2,000 Roman period farms. Dams and other water-control systems also dating to the Roman period were discovered in a number of the seasonal watercourses. They allowed the farmers to produce both cereal crops and olives in areas with very little rainfall. Animals were an important part of the Libyan rural mix, but the use of stalling on farmsteads limited overgrazing. Such rural development was certainly made possible by the increased security of the Pax Romana and was stimulated in part by the Roman tax and market systems. However, those undertaking these improvements appear to have been local tribesmen, not Roman civilian or military settlers.

By the third century AD changes were taking place in the design of the settlements. The *gsur* or fortified farmsteads became more common, but it is unsure whether their increased popularity reflected growing insecurity or the desire to display status through the construction of a tower. Only with the collapse of the Roman political and economic system did the local populace abandon labour-intensive agricultural production for a subsistence system based more on 'bedouin'-style practices. This appears to have been part of a wider process of social and economic change rather than the result of either climate change or any particular political event.

These more recent settlement studies, with their emphasis

on long-term man-land relationships and their strong environmental orientation, have forged closer links between the
archaeologist, geologist and environmental scientist. Geologists
have long been involved in the study of the Roman countryside
both at the site/regional level and on the macro-level. At the
macro-level the geologist provides insight into such problems as
the relationship between climate change and human activities
as manifested in such processes as erosion and deposition. One
of the most important and controversial of such studies, that of
the so-called 'Younger Fill' of late Antiquity, will be discussed in
the last chapter.

The archaeology of the Roman Netherlands provides some
excellent examples of geology applied to problems of the Roman
countryside. It is not surprising that archaeologists working in
the Netherlands would be especially interested in such issues
of man's relationship with the land, for in no other country in
Europe has there been such a complex and long-term symbiotic
relationship between the environment and man. The Netherlands does not have a large number of major Roman rural sites
with impressive architectural remains. Those that once existed
were long ago mined for their building material in a countryside
where stone is very rare. For that reason great effort and
ingenuity has to be employed to extract maximum information
from the exiguous archaeological remains. For this reason
Dutch archaeologists have pioneered the application of a range
of geologically based approaches to archaeology.

A good example of this type of research is that undertaken
by Willem Willems in the territory of the ancient Batavians in
eastern Holland (Willems 1981-84). Willems collected a range
of archaeological evidence from the published literature and
from survey. However, he also employed effectively geological
and geomorphological information. One especially useful tool
was phosphate analysis. Soil phosphate levels are a sensitive
indicator of human activities, and phosphates produced by
human activity remain stable in the soil for long periods of time.

Agricultural land is a precious commodity in Holland, and Dutch agronomists have made extensive, detailed studies of soil chemical compositions including phosphate concentrations. Sites with high phosphate levels were noted on their soil maps. Willems and his colleagues made archaeological soundings at such sites and demonstrated a high level of correlation between the phosphate concentrations and Roman-period occupation. A detailed Roman settlement history for a distinctive region of north-east Europe has been reconstructed in what seems at first to be a very unpromising landscape.

The scientific reconstruction of the vegetation history of the Roman landscape is not nearly as advanced as the geological and geomorphological research. A great deal has been written on such topics as deforestation during the Roman Empire, but usually conclusions are based on anecdotal information in the literary sources. A classic work such as Russell Meiggs' *Trees and Timber in the Ancient Mediterranean World* (1982) relied almost totally on the ancient written sources. Inscriptions, like one from Spain concerned with the designation of a landlot for the specific use of a bath (*CIL* 2.3361) or the tablet recently discovered in London that records a dispute over the ownership of a tract of woodland in Kent (*Britannia* 1994: 302-4), provide more precise insight into Roman woodland management. However, they are still relatively few in number.

Information on changes in the general floral background and on specific crop uses during the Roman period can be obtained from the analysis of pollen from deposits in ponds and swamps, and from the study of seeds and pollen found in specific archaeological contexts. Such research has been employed with good results in prehistoric archaeology, but has been less widely applied to the Roman countryside. The effectiveness of such research is limited by the uneven distribution of pollen samples, especially in the Mediterranean where lakes and swamps are rare. Problems also exist in the dating techniques used in pollen analysis, which are usually too imprecise to provide the historical correlations desired by ancient historians or archaeologists. Pioneering pollen research in lakes of the Ager Veiantanus provided evidence for a reduction of forests during the early third century BC which seems to coincide with the expansion of Roman settlement (Hutchinson 1970; Potter 1979). However, the chronological fix is based on radiocarbon-dating that may have too much of a margin of error to allow such historical associations.

Roman Britain has provided us with some of the best and most diverse botanical profiles for any Roman province, including both pollen and seed studies. Yet even there the picture is very uneven and the number of samples studied, especially for pollen analysis, still relatively small. Many of the most useful pollen profiles have come from bogs and swamps located in areas such as northern Britain where pre-Roman patterns of rural land use persisted, while the good seed samples tend to come more from the villas of the Romanized population than from the native farmsteads.

One of the most important Roman botanical studies is Van der Veen's attempt (1992) to reconstruct the agricultural regimes in the border country behind and beyond Hadrian's wall from the late prehistoric to the Roman period. One development of particular note was the expansion of plough agriculture during the Roman period as compared to that of the Iron Age. The identification of local crop remains at northern British army sites suggests that this expansion of intensive agriculture in the hinterland of the military frontier was related to the needs of the army. A similar situation developed in the hinterland of the Rhine frontier. However, unlike the Rhine frontier, no prosperous villa culture developed in northern Britain. This may have been the result of differences in landscape and society, but may also have been the consequence of more oppressive extractive policies implemented by the army that impoverished the region and prevented the emergence of a diverse rural society.

3. Aerial Photography

The progress in both settlement and environmental archaeology discussed in the last two chapters has certainly deepened
our knowledge of the Roman countryside. It has also made us
appreciate its complexity and diversity. Generalizations such as
the domination of slave-based plantation economy in later Republican Italy have been made increasingly doubtful by the
accumulating archaeological evidence. While the creation of the
Roman political, social and economic world did produce major
changes in the countryside, many local and regional variations
developed. That was true for even the most Romanized parts of
the rural world. However, archaeologists and historians have
increasingly come to appreciate the limits of Roman transformation, especially in the countryside. The limits of Romanization, the strength of the survivals, and the importance of
what one scholar has described as the 'creolization' of the
Roman Empire (Webster 2001) will be the subject of the next
chapter.

4

Resistance and Continuity: An Indigenous Perspective on the Roman Countryside

The dominant tradition in the study of the Roman countryside has been one that stressed the transformations produced by Romanization and denied or downgraded any continuities with the pre-Roman past. This model has been particularly important in the study of the western Roman provinces, where emphasis was placed on the ways in which the Romans transformed the countryside, destroying much of the pre-existing indigenous society and replacing it with Roman forms of social and economic organization. Such an approach to Roman rural society clearly reflected the colonialist world of the provincial archaeologists working in countries such as Britain and France (Hingley 2000).

Such 'imperial' models are no longer accepted in modern colonial studies, and they have been increasingly questioned in Roman history too. Liberation movements directed against modern colonial powers stimulated an interest in ancient resistance movements – both violent uprisings such as that of Boudicca in Britain and longer-lasting guerilla wars such as those of Tacfarinas in North Africa. Ancient historians and archaeologists used anthropological and historical models developed for modern colonial situations to reinterpret indigenous resistance to Rome (Dyson 1971, 1975).

4. Resistance and Continuity

Movements like those of Boudicca and Tacfarinas were ultimately crushed. However, that did not mean a rapid, total domination of indigenous societies by Rome. Students of both modern and ancient colonialism now place great emphasis on the limits and failures of the imperial process. The research of James Scott has highlighted ways in which rural populaces have resisted their modern colonial overlords not by violence, but by placing a series of small but effective obstacles in the way of their imperial oppressors. Another approach that is currently very popular with Romanists emphasizes the limited ability of the Romans to project power and produce change. The Roman Empire was run by a small bureaucracy, almost no police force, and a military stationed mainly on the frontier. New Roman settlements were relatively few. Most of the people living in the countryside were descendants of the pre-Roman inhabitants and retained many of their pre-Roman ways. In this new model, Rome is seen as a 'minimalist' empire in which, if you paid your taxes and kept the peace, you could generally continue to follow your traditional ways.

Certain Roman provinces have lent themselves especially well to these new types of post-colonial researches. Britain, where the Roman conquest of the island had been incomplete and many areas even within the province only partially transformed by the Roman presence, provides a particularly good case-study. Roman Sardinia is another. Sardinia had a long and rich history before the Romans came on the scene. The most striking reminders of that pre-Roman past are the stone towers known as *nuraghi* that are still an omnipresent feature of the Sardinian landscape. Some 7,000 have been documented on the island. Most seem to have been built between the mid-second and the early first millennium BC, when the cultures associated with them flourished. Parts of coastal Sardinian were occupied by the Phoenicians from the eighth century BC, and from the mid-sixth century BC the Carthaginians attempted to establish their control of the island. The extent of their success has been much debated, but it is clear that when the Romans incorporated Sardinia into their Empire in the mid-second century BC, much of the island had been only superficially subdued.

The Romans waged a series of bloody wars aimed at breaking Sardinian resistance. The accepted picture is that these were successful, and the indigenous culture was largely destroyed. Sardinian specialists have long claimed that the *nuraghi* sites were largely abandoned and the Sardinian countryside turned into a land of latifundia that supplied grain to the city of Rome. However, recent survey work has demonstrated that such a colonialist reconstruction is too simplistic. Many *nuraghi* sites were occupied into the late Roman Empire, and the development of villa culture was largely limited to coastal and suburban areas. Although Sardinia has been one of the first overseas provinces taken by Rome, Romanization seems to have been minimal outside of the coastal zone, and many aspects of the pre-Roman way of rural life survived until the collapse of the Empire.

Britain had a much shorter Roman history, but Romano-British archaeologists influenced by their own country's imperial agenda long emphasized the degree to which the province did become Roman. Villa studies were, as we have seen, central to this picture of a province that was to a high degree acculturated. Scholars like Robin Collingwood realized early that this was not the whole picture and that in some areas traditional ways of life continued. However, these were regarded as backward regions, which held relatively little interest for the student of a true Roman province. Only recently have archaeologists working in a more post-colonial paradigm approached this 'other Roman Britain' in a more positive manner.

Their task was aided not only by changes in ideology, but also by new approaches to the rural archaeology of Roman Britain The development of a more comprehensive landscape archaeology, stimulated in part by the needs of Cultural Resource Management, has helped provide much new information on

76

both indigenous survival and the complex cultural mixture in Roman rural Britain. Investigators engaged in archaeological resource studies have to employ field methodologies that provide information on the total universe of archaeological sites in an area and that do not privilege a certain culture or a certain time period. Villages, fields and farmsteads that represent the survival of Iron Age peasants and their traditional ways, or the sheep pens of pastoral societies, must each receive as much attention as the villas of elite Roman provincial society. The impact of such new approaches can be seen in a regions like Cornwall, where over a thousand Roman-period native settlements have been documented, providing insights into a dynamic if simple indigenous society that continued relatively unchanged under the Roman Empire (Hingley 1989).

Even in the villa zone of south-east England, villages and native farmsteads continued in complex relationships with villas. Local differences were considerable. Areas of north Oxfordshire that in the Iron Age supported large communities show little villa development, while other sections in the same micro-region that were characterized by smaller villages or farmsteads units during the Iron Age seem to have embraced the villa economy (Hingley 1989). While the archaeologist cannot always reconstruct social and economic structures from such physical remains, the existence of mixed settlements makes it clear that we have to think about dependent peasantry and share-cropping economies as well as the 'slave-based estate'.

One of the most stimulating recent scholarly controversies has centred on the interpretation of the ground plans of Romano-British villas. Initially, the villa with an organization of space reflecting a Mediterranean lifestyle appeared to be the ultimate expression of Romanization. However, since the days of Haverfield archaeologists have agreed that most Romano-British villas were inhabited by acculturated natives and not by Roman settlers from the continent. Since few such villas have been excavated with careful attention to the intra-site distribution of pottery and other material culture, social structures have to be read from the plans themselves. J.T.S. Smith has argued that more of Celtic social organization can be seen in the planning of villa organization than has generally been thought. The presence of duplicate sets of rooms in Romano-British villas could reflect the survival of Celtic family structures where multiple branches of the same family lived under one roof. However, such connections have to be used with caution. The Romans themselves had multi-generational households and duplicate room suites are common in places like Pompeii.

The large body of new evidence not only on the settlements of classic Roman types, but on those that represent the continuation of pre-conquest forms of habitation and social organization, raise questions about the nature and validity of maps of the Roman countryside. This debate has intensified with the recent publication of the *Barrington Atlas of the Roman World* a brilliant attempt to provide an updated geographical representation of the Roman Empire. The *Barrington Atlas* provides a well documented picture of the Roman world of cities, towns, roads and military sites that will, with limited modification, stand the test of time. The presentation of the countryside is more open to controversy (Alcock, Dey & Parker 2001). Even the scale of the *Atlas*'s generous format allowed for the inclusion of only the larger rural sites. Thus for Sardinia the hundreds if not thousands of *nuraghi* sites known to have been occupied during the Roman period do not appear. A landscape that was in fact full during the Roman Empire appears empty on the map. Such distortions of what was a past reality have a particular impact on our understanding of indigenous survivals in the Roman world, not limited to Sardinia. The problem will be compounded by the continuing increase in our knowledge of the countryside. While relatively few new towns will need to be added, hundreds of new rural sites are discovered each year.

4. Resistance and Continuity

The cartography of the Roman countryside is a field where new electronic mapping techniques such as GIS must soon replace even the best printed atlases and allow us continuously to update our information and regularly modify our visual representations of that new data.

One of the most complex areas of Roman-native cultural interaction was that of rural religion. Cult served the needs of those who lived in and used the resources of the classical countryside in multiple ways. Peasants have always lived with multiple forces outside their control and have always tried to propitiate and control these 'divine' elements by a range of 'religious' acts. The country folk of Roman Italy displayed great religious conservatism, following old cults and practices well into the Christian period. They also appreciated the importance of such cult activities for the peoples of the provinces that they conquered. Since Roman popular religion was highly flexible and pragmatic, it is not surprising that in most areas a multi-cultural dynamic led to a blend of Roman and native practices. The evolution of Roman religion in the provinces should not be seen in terms of dominance and resistance, but rather sympathetic intermingling.

The religion of the Italian countryside before the Roman conquest was not just a collection of peasant cult practices but also an instrument of elite domination. In the mountainous regions of central Italy urbanism was poorly developed and the great sanctuaries provided a focus not only for cult, but also for political, social and economic integration in tribal societies. By the period of Roman expansion in the third and second centuries BC some of these religious centres, like Pietrabbondanze in the Samnite country, had achieved a high level of architectural monumentality with a stone-built theatre and other substantial religious structures. Since the sanctuaries were the focus of elite resistance to Rome, they were attacked by the Romans, especially during the time of the Social War in the early first century BC. Most were destroyed, but a few did remain in use

79

under the Empire. However, they never achieved the wealth and importance enjoyed during the pre-conquest period.

The Romans instead encouraged the development of towns as a focus of elite activity and a replacement for the old sanctuaries with their subversive associations. Religious ceremonies connected first with the traditional Roman deities and then the imperial cult became the special activity of the new ruling class and was key to their integration into Roman society. Many of the towns were agro-towns and drew in the surrounding rural populace for the payment of taxes, for market, but also for religious ceremonials that made them part of the new Roman world.

However, the rural sanctuary did not disappear from the Italian countryside. Pliny the Younger notes its importance for the regions surrounding his Umbrian country estates. He paid special attention to the cult site of Clitumnus and described in some details both the rituals associated with the shrine and his role in it as patron. A good archaeological example of such a rustic sanctuary is that of Feronia in the territory of the Vestini near Pescara. A landslide had buried the temple site in the early third century AD. It was a modest place with a small, single-room temple. Lamps found among its votive deposits show that worship at the shrine continued into the third century AD. One of the more important functions of shrines of Feronia was to provide a sacred setting for the freeing of slaves. A small square pedastal found at this site has been plausibly identified as the place where slaves sat during the manumission process.

The Romans carried the lessons learned from their conquest of Italy into the provinces. Potential foci of resistance such as the 'druid groves' of Anglesey shared the same fate as the shrines of Samnium. The Roman officials used both tradition and religious innovation to integrate the emerging new provincial elite into the Roman system. New towns were established, and each of the provinces had a cult centre that was the focus of rituals of political loyalty. Lyon in France and Colchester in Britain were two such places. In the major towns Roman-style religious activities became an important part of urban life. In the countryside the proprietors of the villas adopted Roman household cults and sponsored religious activities that displayed their identity with the new power.

Outside such distinctly Roman orbits as the town and the villa the reality of provincial religion was clearly more nuanced. An excellent example of the complex relationship between the ongoing traditions of indigenous religion and innovations produced by Romanization was the so-called Romano-Celtic temple. Those temples had a distinctive plan with a square central cella and a surrounding portico. It has been suggested that this plan and especially the use of the surrounding porticos reproduced in more monumental form the Celtic sacred groves with collections of ex-voto offerings. In some cases, such as the sacred complex at Gournay-sur-Aronde in France, the evolution of the cult site can be traced from the Iron Age into the Roman period. However, even there the Roman building was significantly more monumental than any Celtic predecessor. New improved excavations are revealing more examples of Celtic-Roman continuity. However, it is also clear that the period after the Roman conquest saw the building of many new Romano-Celtic temples, especially in south-eastern England and north-western France. What is most striking about the distribution of the English temples is that the highest concentration was in the most Romanized part of the island where the villas were thickest on the ground. The owners of these villas were mostly acculturated Britons, who in their residential lifestyle identified with the conquerors, but in religion pursued innovative blends of native and Roman forms.

One very important result of the systematic application of aerial photography to the countryside of north-eastern France has been the discovery of a large number of previously unknown Romano-Celtic temples, or *fana*, their distinct square forms clearly visible in the cultivated fields. Over forty have been identified in the Picardy area alone, where previously almost none had been known. Many are small, isolated structures, the focus of rural worship for the local district. While some have yielded traces of late Iron Age occupation underneath the Roman remains, the more permanent structures are generally early imperial in date. As in Britain, they were especially common in the villa-dominated countryside. The Romans apparently felt quite comfortable in encouraging the construction of such hybrid religious buildings whose physical setting and presumably religious rituals were more native than Roman.

Most of these *fana* were simple cella-ambulatory structures without associated buildings. However, some were part of much more complex sanctuaries. Again it has been the aerial photographic research in north-eastern France that has provided much of the new information on these larger rural shrines. Some had multiple temples, baths and theatres. These rural theatres, which were quite common in northern Gaul, must have been the foci for religious performances that gathered in the country folk and enhanced the sense of identity between the rural population and the great sanctuaries. Few of the theatres identified by aerial photography have been extensively excavated. However, the history of a theatre-shrine such as that at Canouville in Seine Maritime, built in the mid-second century AD, and abandoned by the late third century seems representative.

One of the largest of these rural shrines was that at Ribemont-sur-Ancre near Amiens. It had a temple complex, theatre, baths and other cult-related structures (Brunaux *et al.* 1999). A Celtic trophy shrine had preceded the Romano-Celtic temple. A large number of skeletons without skulls were found in the shrine, suggesting the sacrifice of prisoners of war. The destruction of the native sanctuary and the construction of the Roman temple were most likely revenge and cleansing acts on the part of the Roman military. The baths were added on in the early second century AD but went out of use in the early third century. The theatre, which had a seating capacity of 3,000, was burned in the third century but restored under Constantine. Some cult activity continued at the shrine until the end of the fourth century AD.

Another large Gallic sanctuary was that at Châteauneuf in Savoy (Mermet 1993). It had a shrine, a theatre, a bath complex, and a habitation quarter. Occupation began in the first century AD and continued well into the fourth century AD. Worship there focused on Mercury and Maia, whose cult activities probably incorporated elements of worship from a pre-existing indigenous deity. The nearly eighty graffiti found scratched on wall plaster, pottery and tiles found in the sanctuary give an insight into the people who worshipped there. The names suggest that most did not belong to the highest social rank.

The study of spring cults provides one of the best examples of the complex interactions between indigenous cultures and Roman forms in both the Mediterranean and north-west Europe. Spring water has always had great importance for the peoples of the parched Mediterranean countryside. Even in areas such as central Gaul and Britain where rainfall was more reliable, the flow of water from the earth was endowed with magical qualities. Special attention was paid to thermal and mineral springs, whose health-promoting qualities had long been recognized.

Since World War II archaeological research has considerably expanded our knowledge of the spring cults of Italy and the western Roman Empire. On the mainland one of the most important was that of the *Aquae Apollinares* at Vicarello near Veii. Its extensive collection of votives included glass goblets with road itineraries inscribed on them, perhaps a thank-offering left by some traveller who had completed the arduous journey from Spain to Italy. In Sardinia, where the inhabitants of a landscape with little rain depend on the numerous springs for survival, worship at sites of 'living water' had a long history. Some of the most impressive examples of *nuraghi* architecture are structures that housed spring cults. The ex-voto material discovered at a number of Sardinian shrines shows that they continued in use under the Romans. The thermal spring 'Aquae Hypsitanae' at Fordongianus in the Tirso river valley was an important sacred spring located at the boundary between the Roman and native spheres. Originally a sacred place where Sards and Romans met for diplomatic negotiations, by the High Empire Fordongianus had become a curative bathing establishment, an instance of 'Vichy replacing Lourdes'.

Spring cults were especially important in Roman Gaul. Two of those located in central France, one at Source-de-la-Seine and a second near Clermont Ferrand, have attracted special archaeological attention, because damp soil conditions at the sites have preserved thousands of wooden votive offerings. The statues at Source-de-la-Seine (Deyts 1983) numbered in the hundreds and included male and female hooded and nude figures, head and body parts and a few animal representations. The styles of the figures ranged from examples of simple folk art with definite Celtic influences to images that clearly showed the influence of classical art and reflect a mixture of indigenous and Roman worshippers. These two sanctuaries reached their greatest prosperity during the early years of the Roman province. Neither appears to predate the Roman conquest, and neither outlived the Julio-Claudian dynasty.

Fordongianus was not the only thermal spring that profited from the combination of health and religion. Bath in southwestern England is a better known example. Recent archaeological excavations at Bath have reconstructed its long cult history and its religious architecture and visual iconography with their complex blends of Roman and Celtic influences. Roman Bath does not seem to have developed into a real town, but remained a spa centre. However, rather like its eighteenth/nineteenth-century successor immortalized by Jane

4. Resistance and Continuity

Austen, it forged an important link between the rural populace and the more Romanized elite.

Post-processual archaeologists have placed increasing emphasis on the need to interpret the landscape, not just as a place of production, but also as a symbolic theatre where historical memory was preserved and various elements in society competed for ideological dominance. Susan Alcock has written perceptively about the landscape of memory that existed in Roman Greece (1993). While the landscape of the Roman West could not have the same deep layering of literary association, similar struggles to dominate its visual ideology must have been played out there through the intersection of oral traditions and visual monuments. Rome could destroy the political and social order of Italians, Celts and Iberians, but it could not totally erase the marks they had impressed upon the landscape. The multi-layered prehistoric landscape of Stonehenge with its centuries of historical associations provided the background for the new Roman settlements on Salisbury Plain. The hillforts of Spain, France and Britain were largely deserted, either sacked by the Roman army or abandoned by their former inhabitants as they converted to the new Roman lifestyle. However, their impressive defences remained visible to the peasants working on the Roman estates below, reminders of the military glories of their ancestors and their resistance against Rome. In rural Sardinia the thousands of *nuraghi* remained omnipresent and dominant man-made presences in a rural landscape that the Romans had altered little.

From the moment of conquest the Romans started to place their physical and symbolic impress on the countryside. The high places of the Roman provincial landscapes were dotted with trophies of arms erected after Roman victories, many decaying but others, like those at the passes of the Alps and the Pyrenees, rebuilt permanently in stone. Roads with their bridges and rhythmic milestones cut across the landscape. As the locals looked down from one of their decaying hillforts on the bold lines of the new roads, they were made very conscious of the dominance of a new order, just as their descendants millennia later would appreciate how the tracks of the railways brought similar changes to the nineteenth-century rural world. Square-built stone and timber structures gradually replaced many of the native farmsteads, and these in turn were replaced by the more imposing architecture of the villas. The stone tower of, for example, Stonea overlooking the Cambridgeshire fens was a visible reminder of the new Roman order for descendants of the Iron Age inhabitants.

The sacred and mortuary landscapes changed as well. Some sacred groves associated with anti-Roman military and religious activities were felled, but the Romans too had their tradition of holy woodlands. Oak pollen has been found at one north Gallic sanctuary, suggesting the continued use of the grove as a place of worship. Increasingly hybrid native-Roman forms expressed syncretic religious values. Gallo-Roman temples were frequently placed on elevated land, making them particularly prominent. In parts of north-east Gaul and Germany, dozens of sacred columns dominated the skyline.

The elite of prehistoric Europe had a long tradition of expressing their power through mortuary monuments. Thousands of mounds and other monuments were visible throughout western Roman Europe. Curiosity and a continued search for treasure would have made both the Romans and their indigenous subjects aware that these were the tombs of deceased great men. In areas such as Numidia in North Africa, the pre-Roman elite had built towered funerary monuments in architectural styles that blended Greek and Punic influences. These survived as reminders of the dynasties and individual leaders who had aided the Roman rise to power.

The Roman ruling class had similar mortuary values, though expressed in different physical forms. Outside the towns the rows of elite tombs linked city and country, while on the estates large funerary monuments proclaimed power and possession.

These tomb monuments often blended the high style of the classical world with imagery that expressed the distinctive values of a rural provincial elite. The many relief sculptures from the mortuary monuments of Roman Gaul and Germany especially embody this complex intersection of values. In the early part of the twentieth century, Emile Esperandieu collected and published many of those Roman period reliefs, scattered in a myriad of local museums. In style those monuments range from examples of pure classical form to others where the visual values seem little changed from the European Iron Age. The subjects include religious and mythological references, but also depictions of the social and economic life of this provincial aristocracy.

An imposing tomb preserved at Igel near Trier embodies many of these qualities. The monument was erected in the middle years of the third century AD by a prosperous local family, the Secundinii. The form was that of a tower tomb. Two very different subjects are depicted in the relief decoration. One is focused on classical myth and especially on themes associated with the afterlife. The others deal with the family, commerce and daily life of the Secundinii. Such prosaic themes represent what scholars refer to as plebeian or popular art and reflect the pride in the activities of agriculture and commerce that characterized Roman rural society in both Italy and the north-western provinces.

However, the pre-Roman monuments could not be ignored and seem to have evoked diverse and changing reactions among the native populations. In Britain, the Romans did not usually try to assert hegemony by building monuments of their own at major pre-Roman sites. The Romano-Britain temple at the Iron Age hill fort at Maiden Castle that had been stormed by the Roman army was something of an exception. However, a number of barrow monuments have yielded Roman period burials and Roman pottery and coins. These Roman artifacts are generally not numerous, and many are relatively late in date. They suggest an indigenous population seeking identity with features on the landscape that in some ways they wished to retain as their own (Dark 1993).

Recent research has made it clear that the old models of Romanization shaped by the filtered experiences of nineteenth-century European imperialism were far too simplistic. Much of the past remained in the Roman countryside. However, there is the equal danger that a fashionable embrace of various forms of post-colonial discourse may swing the pendulum too far in the opposite direction. The Romans were there for a long period of time, and their imperial system contained many social and economic transformative forces. Changes were bound to come to rural as well as urban areas. Some of these changes were forced, but others came willingly and reflected the appeal of many aspects of the Roman imperial complex. The danger is that in romanticizing a pre-conquest past and focusing on the real oppressive aspects of Roman domination, we may forget its real appeals. The thousands of villas in the western provinces are clear indicators of elite acceptance. The coins and red-glazed pottery found in a humble farmhouse show both integration into the Roman market economy and acceptance of the blandishments of Roman consumer culture. Emphasis on extreme positions tends to obscure the degree to which a dialectic developed between Roman and native and helped to create a distinctive new society.

5

The End of the
Roman Countryside

The fall of the Roman Empire has fascinated scholars for centuries. The 'whens and the whys' are constantly being reformulated on the basis of new models of interpretation and new evidence. The countryside has been central to this continuing discussion. The Roman rural world was especially vulnerable to disruption as the Roman military system collapsed and barbarian invaders burst into the Empire. City-dwellers could retreat behind their walls, but the unfortified villas and farmsteads were open to the invaders. To the devastation caused by invaders was added an increasingly oppressive tax system that weighed especially heavily on the peasantry. They in turn were driven into increased dependence on the rural elite. Historians have seen various degrees of connection between this late Roman 'colonate' and the rural social and economic structures of the early Middle Ages.

Recent archaeological research has provided information that should force scholars of late Antiquity and the early Middle Ages to rethink their positions and adopt a more nuanced view of what happened in that transitional era. The time frame has been expanded, with archaeologists finding Roman rural sites that continued to be occupied into the fifth and the sixth centuries and even beyond. Regional and local variations became even more important as the unifying aspects of the Roman system weakened. In one area most traces of Roman rural life may disappear almost totally, while in another the system survived surprisingly intact.

The villa remains central to our picture of that era. The literary texts depict a late Antique rural elite for whom the pursuit of *otium* was still central, and for whom the country estate remained important as both a residential and a productive unit. The image is that of a cultured 'last hurrah' in which the senatorial nobility enjoyed the last pleasures of the civilized life while the whole system collapsed around them. The discovery of opulent late Antique villas in different parts of Italy and the western provinces has corroborated this text-based picture. Just after World War II, a large elegantly decorated villa dating to the late third/early fourth century was excavated at Piazza Armerina in the interior of Sicily. Its many rooms and extensive mosaic decorations made clear that it was the country residence of some member of the Roman elite. The villa was first associated with the late third-century emperor Maximian, but it was more likely the property of an important member of the Roman senate. The mosaics, whose themes ranged from classical mythology to the hunting pursuits of the Roman rural elite, were the products of North African workshops. When it was first discovered, the Piazza Amerina villa was seen as an isolated survivor in the middle of Sicily of a rural civilization that was disappearing in other parts of the Roman Empire. However, in recent years other villas of similar splendour and similar date have been discovered in Sicily, and comparable examples are known from other parts of the Roman Empire.

One such group of large, luxurious villas has been found in a remote area on the north slope of the Pyrenees in south-western France. Although connected to the outside world by river systems that flowed into the Atlantic and possessed of rich pockets of agricultural land, the villas and their owners were certainly far removed from the major centres and crossroads of the Roman Empire. The best known of this group is Montmaurin in the Haute Garonne. Its first occupation phase dated to the first century AD, but the complex was subsequently rebuilt, for the last time in the early fourth century. That more opulent later villa was entered through an elegant semi-circular entrance court worthy of an imperial palace. To the left was a small temple of Romano-Celtic plan, a reminder of long-lasting links to indigenous society. The total complex had nearly two hundred rooms and covered ten acres.

Another of these opulent Pyrenean villas was located at Chiragan, some twenty miles to the east of Montmaurin. The complex included not only the villa itself but also outbuildings with a row of small structures that must have been the houses of the *familia rustica*. Occupation started in the Augustan period, but the period of greatest opulence extended from the second to the fourth centuries AD. The villa was destroyed in the early fifth century. Its most striking feature was the enormous quantity of sculpture found there. Esperandeiu included 120 pieces from Chiragan in his catalogue, ranging from imperial busts to reliefs depicting the labours of Hercules (Hannestad 1994). Most seem to have been acquired by the villa-owner in the fourth century.

More recently, a third major villa has been excavated at Lalonquette in the same general area (Lauffray, Schreyeck & Dupre 1973), its last major building phase dated to the fourth and early fifth centuries AD. New mosaic floors were being installed in the early fifth century, and some occupation continued at least into the early sixth century. There were remains of what seem to have been a small chapel and Christian burials at the site.

Such large late villas were not limited to the Mediterranean and isolated pockets in northern Spain and southern Gaul. A farmstead at Centcelles near Tarragona in eastern Spain was rebuilt as an elegant villa in the fourth century, and by the mid-fourth century may have belonged to one of the Roman emperors. It is unusal in that it preserves ceiling as well as floor mosaics, combining depictions of aristocratic hunts with images drawn from the new iconography of Christianity (Hauschild & Arbeiter 1993). Recently another such villa has been found at El Ruedo near Cordoba in the interior of Andalusia. Occupation started in the first century, but it achieved its greatest elegance in the late third/early fourth century. It also had a large *pars rustica*, but that was largely destroyed by modern construction. Again the later villa was decorated with an elegant and diverse sculpture collection. That phase lasted into the early fifth century, when the site was converted to more humble 'industrial' uses.

In Britain a number of large late villas have been excavated. The island was spared many of the troubles of the late third century that affected Gaul and Germany, and from the Constantinian period onwards a high-status villa culture flourished there. Some of the greatest courtyard villas, such as Bignor in West Sussex, Woodchester in Gloucestershire, and Chedworth in Oxfordshire, reached their apogee during those years. Hoards of silver plate found in the countryside, like that from Mildenhall in Suffolk, provide another insight into the opulent and cultured lifestyle. Even more important are the many mosaics from this late period, such as the Orpheus mosaic at Woodchester and the Dionysiac mosaic at Chedworth. Particular qualities of style and production technique have allowed mosaic experts to reconstruct local and regional styles within late Roman Britain, and reconstruct the activities of mural mosaic workers in specific rural areas, especially in south and south-west England.

Unfortunately, the investigation of many of these late villas in both Britain and the continent took place early in the development of archaeology. Antiquarians focused on the reconstruction of architectural plans and the recovery of works of art and not on the recovery of occupation history through careful stratigraphic excavation and analysis of finds. One of the first late Roman villa excavations to apply high quality archaeology to a late Roman villa was that at Ruoti in Lucania in interior south Italy. Its inland location parallels those at Piazza Armerina in Sicily and Chiragan and Mountmaurin in France. The Ruoti villa proved to have been occupied at least down to the sixth century AD. In the mid-fifth century the villa was rebuilt, and a large apsidal receiving room was added. Such formal receiving halls are known from other late villas such as that at Piazza Armerina. They were the loci for rituals of receiving and entertainment which reinforced the local power basis of this rustic elite.

The archaeologist faces a number of problems in reconstructing the final occupation history of a late villa such as Ruoti. The first relates to what archaeologists call post-depositional processes. Since the final occupation debris is that closest to the surface, its materials are those most likely to have been disturbed or destroyed by later natural and man-made activities at the site. This removal of the latest layers at many sites has led excavators to date the end of occupation too early.

Another impediment to defining late occupation is the diminished quantity and changing nature of the datable material culture. By the end of the fourth century, coins become very rare both in Italy and in provinces like Gaul and Britain. African Red Slip pottery, the major ceramic dating tool for the middle to late Empire, continues to be produced down into the late sixth and even early seventh century. However, the distribution networks contract in sometimes unpredictable ways, and this can particularly affect our ability to date interior rural sites. The amphorae remain an important dating source for the later phases of urban and coastal centres, but again they may not reach the interior sites in the same numbers as earlier in the Empire.

The Ruoti excavations made major breakthroughs in identifying and dating new ceramic types that can help fill the information gap on the transitional period between late Antiquity and the early Middle Ages. The site produced a number of later sealed dumps especially rich in previously little studied pottery types. Particularly important were red-painted wares, which had been found at a number of sites in Italy, but whose significance for dating late occupations in southern Italy had not been appreciated. Joann Freed of the Ruoti excavations demonstrated that these red-painted wares were introduced in the late fourth century and continued in use into the sixth century and probably later. The pottery type was apparently developed as a cheap substitute for African Red Slip, and appears to have filled some of the gaps created by the reduction of availability of the latter type. Its production was not limited to the Ruoti region, for red-painted pottery has now been identified at a number of sites, and it has become a good indicator of later occupation at southern Italian sites

The Ruoti project was also important in that the archaeologists undertook an intensive regional survey that placed the villa in the settlement history of the region (Small 1991). While the survey conditions were far from ideal and the sample of sites recovered relatively small, the investigators were able to employ a range of statistical techniques to compensate for the biases in the survey data and produce a plausible picture of development in the catchment area of the villa. Local settlement peaked in the second century and had declined slightly by the fourth-sixth. Interesting was the shift in ratios between villas and vici. The number was almost equal in the early Empire, but by the mid-late Empire the proportion of vici had increased, suggesting a transition toward village society.

The persistence of high-status villa life with some level of general settlement continuity has been documented by surveys and excavations in Italy and the western Roman Empire. Lucania has produced evidence for a number of other villas and farmsteads occupied at least into the sixth century. On the eastern slopes of the Abruzzi larger villas survived into the sixth and even the seventh century, with some hints of even later occupation (Staffa 2000). Villa sites around Farfa in the upper Tiber valley continued to be occupied into the seventh century. In the Biferno valley the larger villas were still inhabited in the fifth century. Around Pisa and Volterra smaller sites persisted into the fourth century, but by the fifth the larger villas dominate. By contrast the countryside of northern Campania saw an inventory of 138 surveyed sites of the first century AD contract to 27 by the fourth century and four by the sixth. Few sites in the Ager Cosanus remained occupied beyond the late second/early third century.

A great diversity of local and regional rural histories is emerging from the increasing number of excavations and surveys in the western provinces. Roman control of the Iberian peninsula collapsed due to a long series of wars and invasions from 409 to 475. However, that did not necessarily mean the end of the Roman rural system. The villa of Vilauba in Catalunya, Spain provided evidence for a long occupation with a final phase that lasted from the fourth to the seventh century (Jones *et al.* 1982). That fact that the pressing facilities at the villa were repaired and even improved down to the late sixth century AD showed that the owners were still producing for the export market. The somewhat uneven evidence from other Iberian villas suggests that such a late occupation was not unusual (Jones 1988). In some cases the Spanish estates passed into the hands of the church. In 551 a young aristocrat named Vincentius donated land and estate centres to the monastery of Asan in central Tarraconensis (Keay 1988: 215). Many other villas were totally abandoned, while at other sites farmsteads were built over their remains.

The situation in the various Gallic provinces was also very complex. Historians and archaeologists have placed great emphasis on the disruptions in the countryside caused by the wars and invasions of the mid-third century AD. This destruction and abandonment is certainly evident in some areas. In the marginal marsh areas of Belgium and the central river areas of the Netherlands a high percentage of sites was abandoned. Pollen studies show that in some parts of northern Germany and the

Netherlands forests were regenerating by the fourth century, an indication of declining agricultural exploitation. In the plateau areas of north-east France most villas seem to have been abandoned by the late third century. Even in the south of Gaul the countryside around Fréjus saw 90% of the sites abandoned by the end of the third century AD.

However, in other regions occupation continued unbroken or farmsteads and villas were rebuilt after a third-century destruction. Corn-drying ovens, an important indicator of rural activity in northern Europe, increase in numbers during the third century. Around the important late imperial centre of Trier over 70% of the rural sites continued to be occupied. Sometime during this period, some 220 km^2 of the best rural land near Trier were enclosed by a wall and turned into the so-called 'Langmauerbezirk' which was still in the imperial fiscus in the seventh century. Villas with mosaics dating to the fifth century have been discovered.

One of the most intriguing phenomena associated with the end of occupation at many villa sites is the presence of cemeteries amid the ruins of the villas. They have been documented at many sites, from the Lucanian villas of Buccino in southern Italy to the villas of Spain and Gaul (Percival 1976). While the burials contain few datable objects, the contexts generally suggest that the bodies were interned not long after the villa had been abandoned. Some of these villa cemeteries have small chapels associated with them which may explain this previously prohibited invasion of the world of the living by that of the dead. The internments among the ruins suggest that the many villa sites remained a focus for community social activity well after the residence itself had been abandoned. They may have resulted in part from the increasing dependent status of the rural peasantry in late Antiquity, as reflected in the row of small houses built close to the villa at Chiragan.

A recent well publicized example of the villa-cemetery is the infant cemetery found at the villa site of Lugnano in the upper

Tiber valley. The Lugnano villa appears to have been largely abandoned when, in the middle fifth century AD, the site was used as a cemetery for infants. Infant burials are generally underrepresented in any mortuary complex, so the presence of a cemetery devoted to them attracted considerable attention. However, they are attested in other areas such as Roman Britain, and their absence from the mortuary record may reflect in part the poor techniques used in many villa excavations. The lack of grave goods made the precise dating of the Lugnano cemetery difficult. However, it seems to have been in use for a relatively short period of time. The excavators have suggested the spread of malaria may have accounted for this apparent increase in local infant mortality. Such associations between the increase of malaria and the abandonment of the Roman countryside in the Mediterranean are hardly new. However, malaria is difficult to document in the archaeological record including the osteological one, and one must be cautious about such a model of demographic disaster based on very limited documentation.

The revival of arguments blaming malaria for the collapse of the Roman rural system raises the question of other natural causes. Plague is always one possible factor, especially since a major pandemic ravaged the Mediterranean during the reign of Justinian. However, it is by no means clear that the Justinianic plague had anything like the destruction staying power of the fourteenth-century Black Death. Until a great deal more mortuary archaeology is done in the Mediterranean, disease-based explanations will have to be used with great caution.

The increase in insect-borne maladies such as malaria is often related to changes in the natural environment, especially the increase of coastal swamps and marshes. This brings us back to arguments proposed by Claude Vita-Finzi in his classic work, *The Mediterranean Valleys* (1969). Vita-Finzi documented a pattern of significant erosion and deposition activity which he designated the 'Younger Fill' and dated to late Antiquity. The causes might be as diverse as deforestation, the breakdown of agricultural terraces as farmers abandoned their fields, or increased rainfall. The alluvium blocked streams and rivers and led to the development of the swamps and marshes that became breeding-grounds for the malarial mosquito.

Archaeologists remain sceptical about connections between this 'Younger Fill' and the decline of the late Antique countryside. It has become increasingly clear that the 'Younger Fill' phenomenon embraces a range of different events scattered not only over a wide geographical area but also over a relatively long period of time. There are also questions of cause and effect. Did the geomorphological changes evidenced by the 'Younger Fill' produce the environmental preconditions for Roman rural decline, or did the decline of the Roman agrarian system and the abandonment of orchards and farmsteads lead to the collapse of terraces, dikes and dams? That in turn would have accelerated processes of erosion and alluviation that led to the collection of the 'Younger Fill'.

The Roman Empire was gradually becoming Christian. The process of conversion had started in the cities and only gradually affected the countryside. However, by the fourth century the changes were affecting rural areas as well. The elite was slowly converting to Christianity, and some retired to their country estates to embrace a semi-monastic lifestyle. As one would expect, some villas became sites of Christian worship. Roman Britain, the most remote of the provinces, has provided several attestations of Christianity at villa sites, including a Christian burial chapel at Lullingstone in Kent and an unambiguous Christian mosaic from Hilton St Mary in Dorset.

This passage from pagan villa to Christian church/monastery is well attested in the literary sources, but has only recently begun to be securely documented in the archaeological record. The great Carolingian monastery at San Vincenzo al Volturno in the Molise was built over the remains of a major Roman villa, where occupation continued down into the sixth century AD. At Farfa the remains of the villa are less evident, but there seems no question that Roman structures underlay the monastery. Rescue excavations at St Giusto in Apulia revealed a villa with a long occupation that remained in use into the sixth century AD. Two wine presses with a capacity of 36,000 litres were installed at that late date, again showing production for external markets. In the middle years of the fifth century AD a church complex with narthex and baptistery was built adjacent to the villa. A second church was added later in the century, apparently as a burial church, for a number of graves were found within its walls. The emphasis on wine production in the last stages of the villa suggests that the estate was now part of the church lands. The clergy didn't need the elegant *pars urbana* but continued to organize the economic activities of the local Christian peasantry who buried their dead within the walls of the church.

While many non-villa sites were abandoned, others saw continued occupation. Again the decreasing amount and generic nature of the material culture makes identification and dating difficult. The problems are compounded by the increased use of ephemeral construction materials, such as wood, which are not easy to identify archaeologically. Since scholars assumed little occupation continuity between late Antiquity and the early Middle Ages they were not sensitive to the possibility of exiguous remains that would document ongoing activity at a site. Fortunately more archaeologists are becoming sensitive to the possibilities of such continuities, and through careful excavation they are finding more and more evidence for later and later occupations at classical sites. John Moreland at San Donato near Farfa uncovered stratified sequences that extended life at the site from the sixth to the eighth century AD. Timothy Potter's team at the site of Monte Gelato north of Rome identified wooden structures dated to the sixth and seventh centuries AD. The ideological, social and economic structures of the countryside changed from late Antiquity to the Middle Ages, but archaeology is increasingly demonstrating that many aspects of life and work continued.

North Africa and Britain provide two very different case-studies of these complex processes of transition that took place from the fifth to the seventh century. In North Africa the major shaping historical events were the Vandal invasion of the fifth century, the Byzantine re-conquest of the sixth century, and the Islamic takeover during the late seventh and early eighth centuries. The archaeological evidence for late Roman North Africa has increased enormously in recent years. As in other regions, this new research in North Africa has demonstrated the many complexities and the extent of regional variation that characterize the transition from the Roman to the Islamic period.

Fortunately for the field archaeologist, North African potteries continued to produce quantities of the African Red Slip ceramics that are the main dating tool for sites of the late Roman Empire in the western Mediterranean. Shipping amphorae also continued to have wide distributions, which is especially important for survey archaeology. Surveys in southern Numidia and Byzacena showed patterns of dense habitation in the fifth and sixth centuries but extensive abandonment by the seventh century. The Kasserine survey documented occupation at many sites that continued well into the fifth century (Hitchner 1989). Studies of rural finds of amphorae show that their distribution actually seems to increase during the Vandalic period. This new archaeological information on Vandalic economy and society matches that provided by the Albertini tablets, a cache of rural economic documents dating to the period, found near the Algerian-Tunisian border just after World War II. The tablets, which come from the heart of the olive oil zone, document what seem to be normal sales of land, olive trees and water control systems (Mattingly 1989). They demonstrate clearly that the arrival of the Vandals in North Africa had a minimal impact. Elements of the rural elite changed, but many core social and economic structures remained intact.

In almost every way the end of Roman Britain forms a total contrast with the end of Roman North Africa. The Roman army and Roman officials departed very expeditiously from the island early in the fifth century. Most contact was lost with the core Roman Empire, coinage disappeared, and the flow of datable trade goods decreased sharply. Invaders with relatively little Roman acculturation began arriving relatively soon. In North Africa the archaeologist deals with a complicated, well documented process that extended over nearly three centuries. In Britain the evidence is slight, but most have regarded any trace of the Roman province as gone within a century.

Recent archaeological research has nuanced this rather stark picture. It appears that for much of the fourth century rural life continued relatively undisturbed. As has already been seen, a rich villa culture continued in many areas of the south. Surveys in north-west Essex showed 86% of the sites occupied in the later fourth century. To the north the villa system expanded in the later fourth century, although in general few new villas were built after the mid-century. Pottery production remained high throughout the century.

The official abandonment of the island resulted in more than the removal of soldiers and bureaucrats. The end of cash tax collection undermined the monetary system and spurred the collapse of the market economy. Even pottery production ended relatively quickly. Recent research has documented some occupation in the towns during the fifth century, but it was on the whole a wretched presence. Almost all villas were abandoned and there is little trace of activities at their sites beyond the early fifth century AD. The base rural population probably did not disappear, although the lack of datable artifacts does not allow us to document them any more than we can document the elite. Pollen studies suggest that there was no drastic decline in cleared land in the fifth century. There were probably shifts in the patterns of land worked, but no massive demographic decline. By the end of the fifth century Mediterranean imports such as African Red Slip pottery appear again in the hillforts of western Britain. However, by this time Roman Britain was dead, and the gaudy glazed objects graced the rituals of a newly emerging indigenous culture, just as their predecessors had done for the Celts before the Romans came on the scene.

Conclusion: Towards a New Vision of the Roman Countryside

Three major paradigms on the Roman countryside of the Mediterranean are currently dominant. The first was that articulated in Ferdinand Braudel's *The Mediterranean and the Mediterranean World in the Age of Phillip II* (1949). Braudel stressed similarities and continuities across the Mediterranean, the importance of the common environment and the dominance of long-term processes, the *longue durée*, in shaping Mediterranean history. The second developed around the theories of Marx, Engels, and later Marxist thinkers such as Moses Finley, and emphasized the centrality of economic and social processes shaped by class conflict. Theirs is the world of Tiberius Gracchus and Spartacus.

Recently, Peregrine Horden and Nicholas Purcell have articulated a new vision of Mediterranean history in their *The Corrupting Sea* (2000). They feel that more stress should be placed on the diversity of Mediterranean history, a diversity shaped by a complex combination of local environment, local social and economic structures, and local histories. Their book has met with a very mixed reception, but it does capture better my own vision of what happened in the Roman countryside, both in the Mediterranean and in the Roman world beyond the Mediterranean.

Current research on the Roman countryside can lead to a variety of not easily reconciled conclusions. Some would argue that there is no such thing as a 'Roman countryside'. Others would see a whole variety of Roman countrysides, many of them mutually exclusive. Certainly the stereotypical world of villas and slaves as a total summation of the Roman countryside is no more valid than white porticoed plantation houses and singing slaves picking cotton would be for capturing the complexity of rural society in the American South before the Civil War. Archaeological research has written into the Roman countryside a whole range of previously neglected factors and demonstrated the great diversity of rural structures over time and space.

Still, it can be argued that certain common processes shaped the Roman countryside throughout all areas of the Empire considered in this book. In every region the building of Roman roads opened up rural areas in a way that they would not be opened up again until the construction of the railways. People, goods and ideas circulated with an ease not found again until the nineteenth century. Rome imposed upon all the Empire except Italy a tax system that weighed most heavily on the countryside. Land-owners and peasants had to produce surpluses that could be sold on the market economy so that they could render unto Caesar.

At the same time, Roman mercantile entrepreneurs did much to encourage the production and circulation of goods that most elements in rural society could afford. *Terra sigillata*, African Red Slip pottery, lamps and glass, to take just a few examples, represented the products of a consumer economy not matched until that of England in the mid-eighteenth century. Such items were found not only in the towns and luxury villas, but also in the humble abodes of the countryside. Indeed we only know about this 'other' Roman countryside because it did literally buy into the Roman system. The circulation of such goods was aided by the development of a sophisticated and flexible system of coinage. Finds of coins in a variety of sites in the countryside make it clear that the rural areas were well tied into that monetary system.

Conclusion

Both the ideology and the reality of Romanization have been the subject of heated debates in recent years. I would certainly agree that arguments for the systematic and deliberate imposition of Roman values and beliefs especially in the countryside do not reflect ancient reality. The Romans had neither the means nor the intent totally to alter rural society. They were pragmatists and they operated with more flexibility and modes of acceptance than most modern imperial systems. Pay your taxes and keep the peace, and the Romans would to a large degree leave you alone.

As one student of Roman native relations has observed, 'the Romans could not force people to buy *terra sigillata*'. However, buy it they did, and that is an often forgotten appeal of Rome. Perhaps one should see ancient Rome not in French or British political imperial terms, but in those of American commercial imperialism. The Romans produced a variety of lifestyle options with appeal for all, whether it was a villa with bath, mosaic and wall-paintings or a single African Red Slip bowl to display beside the traditional hearth. Each such item produced changes big and small.

Countrysides have historically been both violent and conservative places. The citizens of cities could retreat behind their walls, but the peasants of the rural areas were exposed to the devastations of passing armies and the depredations of bandits. Certainly the Roman countryside was not one of total peace, as the literary evidence for bandits and the archaeological evidence for violent destruction make clear. However, there was historically a relatively high level of peace, and that allowed the country dwellers to go about their business, investing, saving and spending in a way that would not be possible in less secure times.

The emphasis placed on tradition and conservation in the Roman countryside has led us to underestimate how dynamic and changing it really was. Certainly students of rural Rome have tended to overestimate the role of villas in society and

105

economy, but we should not go to the other extreme and ignore the tens of thousands of villas and Romanized country homes that were constructed during the centuries of the Pax Romana. Modes of production changed. The recent discoveries of hundreds of rural pottery kilns, not just the great works like those of southern and central Gaul, but also small production centres aimed at local and regional markets, show rural people producing more than just wheat, sheep and pigs.

Some core beliefs remained, but others changed. In most areas a pre-conquest native coming back to his rural world in the second century AD would have found little familiar in the world of worship. Architecture and iconographic representation had changed, although the basic needs met by rural religion were probably the same. What the evidence from religion in the countryside demonstrates best is the creative synthesis that took place there. The face-off between imperialists and post-colonialists has sometimes led scholars to miss the process of blending and integration, of what Jane Webster has called 'creolization', which created a new society that was one of the most impressive achievements of Rome.

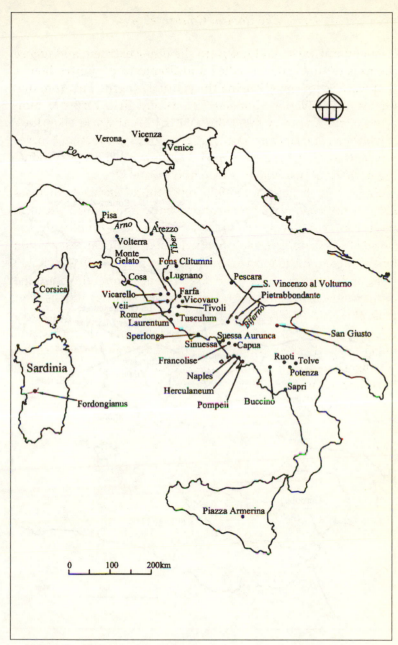

1. Sites in Italy mentioned in the text.

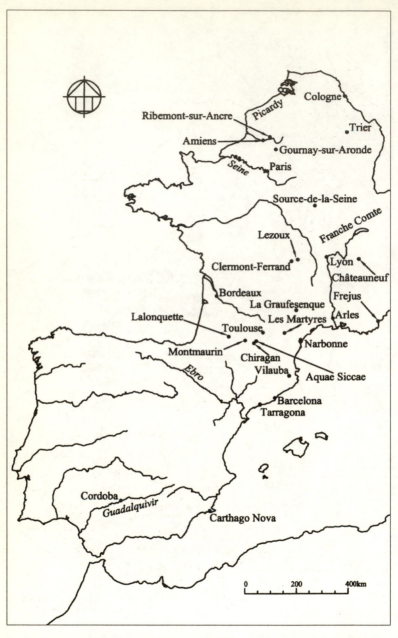

2. Sites in France and the Iberian peninsula mentioned in the text.

3. Sites in Great Britain mentioned in the text.

109

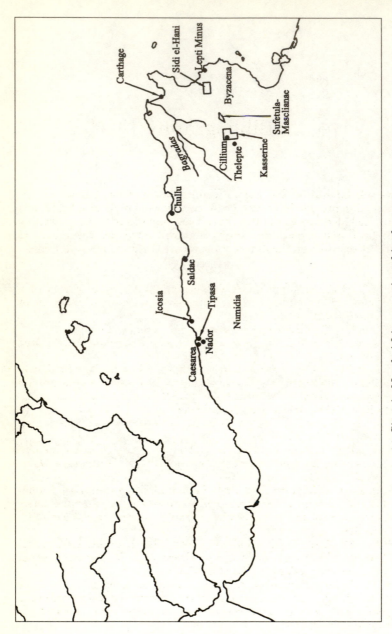

4. Sites in North Africa mentioned in the text.

Bibliography

The scholarship on the Roman countryside is vast. I have not attempted to provide full coverage in the following bibliography. What I have included are works that have been important to me in writing this book and articles and books that will introduce the reader to current research on the different aspects of the Roman countryside.

Abdy, R., R.A. Bunning and C.J. Webster 2001 'The discovery of a Roman villa at Shapwick and its Severan hoard of 9238 silver *denarii*', *JRA* 14: 359-71.

Agache, R. 1978 *La Somme pré-romaine et romaine* Amiens.

de Alarcao, J. 1988 *Roman Portugal*, vol. 1: *Introduction* Warminster, England.

Albarella, U., V. Ceglia and P. Roberts 1993 'S. Giacomo degli Schiavoni (Molise): an early fifth century AD deposit of pottery and animal bones from central Adriatic Italy', *PBSR* 61: 157-230.

Alcock, S. 1993 *Graecia Capta* Cambridge.

Alcock, S., H. Dey & G. Parker 2001 'Sitting down with the Barrington Atlas', *JFA* 14: 454-61.

Allen, J.R.L. & M.G. Fulford 1987 'Romano-British settlement and industry in the wetlands of the Severn estuary', *Antiquaries Journal* 67: 237-74.

Allen, J.R.L. & M.G. Fulford 1990 'Romano-British wetland reclamation at Longney, Gloucestershire and evidence for the early settlement of the inner Severn estuary', *Antiquaries Journal* 70: 288-326.

Arthur, P. 1991 'Territories, wine and wealth: Suessa Aurunca, Sinuessa, Minturnae and the *Ager Falernus*', in *Roman Landscapes* ed. G. Barker & J. Lloyd. London: 153-9.

Arthur, P. 1991a *Romans in Northern Campania* London.

Attolini, I. ed. 1982 'Ricognizione archeologica dell'Ager Cosanus e nella valle dell'Albegna: rapporto preliminare 1981', *Archeologia Medievale* 10: 439-65.

Bibliography

Baden, O., J.P. Brun & G. Conges 1996 'Les bergeries romaines de la Crau d'Arles', *Gallia* 52: 263-310.

Banaji, J. 2001 *Agrarian Change in Late Antiquity: Gold, Labour and Aristocratic Dominance* Oxford.

Baradez, J. 1949 *Fossatum Africae* Paris.

Barker, G. 1989 'The Italian landscape in the first millennium AD: some archaeological approaches' in *The Birth of Europe* ed. K. Randsborg. Rome: 62-73.

Barker, G. ed. 1995 *A Mediterranean Valley* Leicester.

Barker, G. ed. 1995a *The Biferno Valley Survey: The Archaeological and Geomorphological Record* Leicester.

Barker, G & J. Lloyd eds 1991 *Roman Landscapes: Archaeological Survey in the Mediterranean Region* London.

Barker, G., J. Lloyd & D. Webley 1978 'A Classical landscape in Molise', *PBSR* 46: 35-51.

Barker, G., D. Gilbertson & D. Mattingly eds 1996 *Farming the Desert: the UNESCO Libyan Valleys Archaeological Survey* 2 vols Paris/London.

Bayard, D. & J-L. Cadoux 1982 'Les termes du sanctuaire Gallo-Romaine de Ribemont-sur-Ancre (Somme)', *Gallia* 40: 83-105.

Benabou, M. 1975 *La resistance africaine à la romanisation* Paris.

Bentmann, R. & M. Muller 1992 *The Villa as Hegemonic Architecture* Atlantic Highlands, NJ.

Bergès, G. (1989) *Les lamps de Montans (Tarn)* Paris.

Bergmann, B. 1995 'Visualizing Pliny's villas', *JRA* 8:406-20.

Biddick, K. 1989 *The Other Economy* Berkeley & Los Angeles.

Blake, E. 1996 'Negotiating nuraghi: settlement and construction of ethnicity in Roman Sardinia', *TRAC 96* 113-19.

Blanchard-Lemce, M., 1981 'La villa à mosaïques de Mienne-Marboue (Eure et Loir)', *Gallia* 39: 63-83.

von Blanckenhagen, P., M.A. Cotton & J.B. Ward-Perkins 'Two Roman villas at Francolise, Prov. Caserta. Interim Report on Excavations, 1962-64', *PBSR* 33: 55-69.

Bodel, J. 1997 'Monumental villas and villa monuments', *JRA* 10: 5-35.

Bourgeois, A., J. Pugol, J-P. Seguret 1993 'Le sanctuaire gallo-romaine des Baziols à Saint-Beauzoly (Aveyron)', *Gallia* 50:139-80.

Bradford, J. 1957 *Ancient Landscapes* London.

Brandt, R. & J. Slofatra 1983 *Roman and Native in the Low Countries: Spheres of Interaction* Oxford.

Branigan, K. 1994 'The new Roman Britain – a view from the West Country', *Transactions of the Bristol and Gloucestershire Archaeological Society* 112: 9-16.

Branigan, K. & M.J. Dearne 1992 *Romano-British Cavemen* Oxford.

Branigan, K. & D. Miles eds 1989 *The Economics of Romano-British Villas* Sheffield.

Bibliography

Braudel. F. 1976 *The Mediterranean and the Mediterranean World in the Age of Philip II* New York.

Broadribb, A.C.C., A.R. Hands & D.R. Walker 1971 *Excavations at Shakenoak* Oxford.

Brown, F.E. 1980 *Cosa: the Making of a Roman Town* Ann Arbor, Michigan.

Brun, J.P., G.B. Rogers, R. Columeau & M. Thinon 1989 'La villa gallo-romaine de Sainte-Michel à la Garde (Var). Un domaine oleicole au Haut-Empire', *Gallia* 46: 103-62.

Brunaux, J-L. et al. 1999 'Ribemont-sur-Ancre (Somme)', *Gallia* 56: 177-283.

Burnham, B. & J. Wacher 1990 *The Small Towns of Roman Britain* Berkeley.

Cadoux, J.L. 1978 'Un sanctuaire gallo-romain isolé: Ribemont-sur-Ancre (Somme)', *Latomus* 37: 325-57.

Campi, F. 2000 'Pottery and territory: a tormented relationship' in *Extracting Meaning from Ploughsoil Assemblages* ed. R. Francovich, H. Patterson & G. Barker. Oxford: 174-84.

Capogrossi Colognesi, L. 2000 *Max Weber e le economie del mondo antico* Bari.

Carandini, A., ed. 1985 *La romanizzazione dell'Etruria: il territorio di Vulci* Milan.

Carandini, A. 1985a *Settefinestre: una villa schiavistica nell'Etruria romana* Modena.

Carandini, A. & F. Cambi 2002 *Paesaggi d'Etruria* Rome.

Carandini, A. & S. Settis 1979 *Schiavi e padroni nell'Etruria romana* Bari.

Cherry, D. 1998 *Frontier and Society in Roman North Africa* Oxford.

Chouquer, G., M Clavel-Levêque, F. Favory & J-P. Vallat 1987 *Structures agraires en Italie centro-meridionale* Rome.

Claridge, A. 1997-8 'The villas of the Laurentine shore', *Rend. della Pont. Accad. Rom. d'Arch* 70: 307-17.

Clarke, S. 1990 'The social significance of villa architecture in Celtic north west Europe', *Oxford Journal of Archaeology* 9: 337-53.

Clarke, S. 1997 'Social change and architectural diversity in Roman period Britain', *TRAC 97*: 28-41.

Clavel-Levêque, M. ed. 1983 *Cadastres et espace rural: approches et réalités antiques* Paris

Colicelli, A. 1998 'Paesaggio rurale e trasformazione economiche nei Bruttii in età romana', *RdA* 22:113-32.

Conges, A.R. 1997 'La fortune éphémère de Glanum: du religieux à l'économique', *Gallia* 54: 157-202.

Cotton, M.A. 1979 *The Late Republican Villa at Posto, Francolise* London.

Cotton, M.A. & G.P.R. Metraux 1985 *The San Rocco Villa at Francolise* Rome.

113

Courtois, C., L. Leschi, C.H. Perrat & C.H. Saumagne 1952 *Les tablettes Albertini* Paris.

Cronon, W. 1983 *Changes in the Land* New York.

Crumley, C.L. & W.H. Marquand eds 1987 *Regional Dynamics: Burgundian Landscapes in Historical Perspectives* San Diego.

Culot, M. & P. Pinon 1982 *La Laurentine et l'invention de la villa romaine* Paris.

Cunliffe, B. 1971 *Excavations at Fishbourne* Leeds.

Cunliffe, B. & P. Davenport 1985 *The Temple of Sulis Minerva at Bath I: The Site* Oxford.

Dark, K. 1993 'Roman-period activity at prehistoric ritual monuments in Britain and in the Armorican peninsula', *TRAC* 1: 133-46.

Dark, K. & P. Dark 1997 *The Landscape of Roman Britain* Phoenix Mill, Gloucestershire.

D'Arms, J. 1970 *Romans on the Bay of Naples* Cambridge, Mass.

Day, J. 1932 'Agriculture in the life of Pompeii', *Yale Classical Studies* 3: 165-208.

Decombeix, P.M., C. Domerque, J-M. Fabre, A. Gorgiou, C. Ricco, F. Tollon & B. Tournier 2000 'Réflexions sur l'organisation de la production du fer à l'époque romaine dans le basin supérieur de la Dure au voisinage des Martyres (Aude)', *Gallia* 57: 23-36.

De Light, L. 1993 *Fairs and Markets in the Roman Empire* Amsterdam.

De Maria, S. 1991 'Bologna (*Bononia*) and its suburban territory', *Roman Landscapes* ed. G. Barker & J. Lloyd. London: 96-105.

Derks, T. 1998 *Gods, Temples, and Ritual Practices: The Transformation of Religious Ideas and Values in Roman Gaul* Amsterdam.

Deyts, S. 1983 *Les bois sculptés des Sources de la Seine* (XLII supplément à *Gallia* Paris.

Dietz, S., L.L. Sebai & H. Ben Hassen eds 1995 *Africa proconsularis: Regional Studies in the Segermes Valley of Northern Tunisia*, vols 1-2. Aarhus.

Dilke, O.A.W. 1971 *The Roman Land Surveyors* New York.

Di Mino, M.R.S. & A.R. Staffa 1995-97 'Il santuario italico-romano della Dea Feronia in località Poggio Ragone di Loreto Aprutino (PE)', *Atti Pont. Acad.* 69: 155-86.

Dore, J.N. 1985 'Settlement chronology in the pre-desert zone: the evidence of the fine wares', *Town and Country in Roman Tripolitania* ed. D. Buck & D.J. Mattingly. Oxford: 107-25.

Dunbabin, K. 1978 *The Mosaics of Roman North Africa* Oxford.

Duncan Jones, R. 1982 *The Economy of the Roman Empire: Quantititive Studies* Cambridge.

DuPrey, P. 1994 *The Villas of Pliny from Antiquity to Posterity* Chicago.

Duval, N. 1985 'L'iconographie des "villes africaines" et la vie rurale dans l'Afrique romaine de l'Antiquité Tardive', *Actes du IIIe Colloque sur l'Histoire et l'Archéologie de l'Afrique du Nord* Montpellier: 163-76.

Bibliography

Dyson, S.L. 1971 'Native revolts in the Roman Empire', *Historia* 20: 239-74.

Dyson, S.L. 1975 'Native revolt patterns in the Roman Empire', *Aufstieg und Niedergang der römischen Welt*, vol. 2.3 ed. H. Temporini & W. Haas. Berlin: 138-75.

Dyson, S.L. 1978 'Settlement patterns in the *Ager Cosanus*: the Wesleyan University Survey', *JFA* 5: 251-68.

Dyson, S.L. 1983 *The Roman Villas of Buccino* Oxford.

Dyson, S.L. 1992 *Community and Society in Roman Italy* Baltimore.

Dyson, S.L. & R.J. Rowland jr. 1992 'Survey and settlement and reconstruction in west-central Sardinia', *AJA* 96: 203-24.

Edis, R. 1990 'The Byzantine era in Tunisia: a forgotten footnote?', *Journal of North African Studies* 4: 45-61.

Esperandieu, E. 1910-1938 *Recueil général des bas-reliefs, statues et bustes de la Gaule romaine* Paris.

Evans, J. 1990 'From the end of Roman Britain to the "Celtic West" ', *Oxford Journal of Archaeology* 9: 91-103.

Evans, J. 1998 'Crambeck: the development of a major northern pottery industry' in *The Crambeck Roman Pottery Industry* ed. P.R. Wilson. York: 43-90.

Fauduet, I. & D. Bertin 1993 *Atlas des sanctuaires romano-celtique de Gaule* Paris.

Favory, F. & J-L. Fiche 1994 *Les campagnes de la France méditerranéenne dans l'Antiquité et le haut Moyen Âge* Paris.

Fentress, E. 1999 'Villa, vicus, pieve, castrum: the valley of the Treia in the first millennium AD', *JRA* 12: 799-805.

Fentress, E. & P. Perkins 1988 'Counting African red slip ware', *L'Africa Romana* 5: 205-14.

Fentress J. & E. 2001 'Review article: the hole in the dnut', *Past & Present* 173: 205-19.

Ferdière, A. 1988 *Les campagnes en Gaule romaine* Paris.

Fernández Castro, M.C., 1982 *Villas romanas en España* Madrid.

Fiches, J-L. 1987 'L'espace rural antique dans le sud-est de la France: ambitions et réalités archéologique', *Annales ESC* 42.1: 219-38.

Fincham, G. 1999 'Romanisation, status and the landscape: extracting a discrepant perspective from survey data', *TRAC 99*: 30-5.

Finley, M.I. 1983 *Ancient Slavery and Modern Ideology* Harmondsworth.

Finley, M.I. 1985 *The Ancient Economy* 2nd ed. London.

Finley, M.I. 1986 'Archaeology and history' in *The Use and Abuse of History* London: 87-101.

Forcey, C. 1997 'Whatever happened to the heroes? Ancestral cults and the enigma of Romano-Celtic temples', *TRAC 97*: 87-98.

Fouet, G. 1969 *La villa gallo-romaine de Montmaurin (Haute Garonne)* Paris.

Bibliography

Fracchia, H. & M. Gualtieri 1998/99 'Roman Lucania and the Upper Bradano Valley', *MAAR* 43/44: 295-343.

Fredericksen, M.W. 1970-1 'The contribution of archaeology to the agrarian problem in the Gracchan period', *Dial. di Arch.* 4-5: 330-57.

Freed, J. 1983 'Pottery from the late Middens at San Giovanni', *Lo scavo di S. Giovanni di Ruoti ed il periodo tardoantico in Basilicata, Atti dell Tavola Rotonda-Roma, 4 Luglio 1981* ed. M. Gualtieri, M. Salvatore & A. Small. Bari: 91-106.

Frere, S. & J. St Joseph 1983 *Roman Britain from the Air* 1983.

Frischer, B & I.G. Brown 2001 *Allen Ramsey and the Search for Horace's Villa* London.

Gilbertson, D., C. Hunt & G. Gillmore 2000 'Success, longevity, and failure of arid-land agriculture: Romano-Libyan floodwater farming in the Tripolitanean pre-desert', *The Archaeology of Drylands* ed. G. Barker & D. Gilbertson, London: 137-59.

Gilkes, O.J., A. King & A. French 1999 'From *villa* to *village*: ceramics and Late Antique settlement in the Sabina Tiberina', *Archeologia medievale* 26: 269-77.

Gorges, J.G., 1979 *Les villas hispano-romaines* Bordeaux.

Green, M.J. 1976 *A corpus of religious material from the civilian areas of Roman Britain* Oxford.

Green, M.J.1999 *Pilgrims in Stone* Oxford.

Greene, K. 1986 *The Archaeology of the Roman Economy* Berkeley.

Gsell, S. 1911 *Atlas archéologique de l'Algérie* Algiers/Paris.

Gualtieri, M. 2000 'Il territorio della Basilicata nord-orientale', *L'Italia meridionale in età tardo antica: Attti XXXVIII Convegno di studi sulla Magna Grecia 1998:* 369-90.

Haley, E.W. 1996 'The land as map: problems of Roman land division in Baetica', *Classical Bulletin* 72: 19-28.

Hannestad, N. 1994 *Tradition in Late Antique Sculpture* Aarhus.

Hauschild, T. & A. Arbeiter 1993 *La villa romana de Centecelles* Barcelona.

Haverfield, F. 1912 *The Romanisation of Roman Britain* Oxford.

Hawthorne, J.W.J. 1996 'Post-processual economics: the role of African Red Slip Ware vessel volume in Mediterranean demography', *TRAC 96*: 29-37.

Hayes, J.W. 1972 *Late Roman Pottery* Rome.

Hingley, R. 1989 *Rural Settlement in Roman Britain* London.

Hingley, R. 2000 *Roman Officers and English Gentlemen* London.

Hitchner, R.B. 1989, 'The organization of rural settlement in the Cillium-Thelepte region (Kasserine, Central Tunisia)', *L'Africa romana* 6: 387-402.

Hitchner, R.B. 1995 'The culture of death and the invention of culture in Roman Africa', *JRA* 8:493-8.

Hitchner, R.B. 1997 'A tale of two African surveys', *JRA* 10: 567-70.

Bibliography

Hitchner, R.B. 2000 'Gauls into Romans? The making of Gauls under the Roman Empire', *JRA* 13: 611-14.

Hitchner, R.B. & D.J. Mattingly 1991 'Ancient agriculture', *National Geographic Research and Exploration* 7(1): 56-69.

Hodges, R. 2000 *Visions of Rome: Thomas Ashby, Archaeologist* London.

Hodges, R. et al. 1984 'Excavations at Vaccareccia (Rochetta Nuova): a later Roman and early medieval settlement in the Volturno valley, Molise', *PBSR* 52: 148-94.

Hodges, R. & J. Mitchell, eds 1985 *San Vincenzo al Volturno: The Archaeology, Art and Territory of an Early Medieval Monastery* Oxford.

Hodges, R. & D. Whitehouse 1989 *Mohammed, Charlemagne, and the Origins of Europe* London.

Horden, P. & N. Purcell 2000 *The Corrupting Sea* Oxford.

Howgego, C. 1994 'Coin circulation and the integration of the Roman economy', *JRA* 7: 5-21.

Hutchinson. G.E. ed. 1970 'Ianula: an account of the history and development of the Lago di Monterosi', *Transactions of the American Philosophical Society* n.s. 60, pt. 4.

Jackson, R.P.J. & T.W. Potter 1996 *Excavations at Stonea, Cambridgeshire, 1980-85* London.

Johns, C.M. 'The classification and interpretation of Romano-British treasures', *Britannia* 27:1-16.

Johnson, P. 1987 *Romano-British Mosaics* Aylesbury.

Jones, B. 2000 'Aerial archaeology around the Mediterranean', *Non-Destructive Techniques Applied to Landscape Archaeology* ed. M. Pasquinucci & F. Trement. Oxford 49-60.

Jones, G.D.B. 1984 ' "Becoming different without knowing it". The role and development of *vici*', *Military and Civilian in Roman Britain* ed. T.F.C. Blagg & A.C. King. Oxford: 75-91.

Jones, R.F. J. 1988 'The end of the Roman countryside in the Iberian peninsula', *First Millennium Papers* ed. R.F.J. Jones, J.H.F. Bloemers, S.L. Dyson & M. Biddle. Oxford: 159-73.

Jones, R.F.J, S.J. Keay, J.M. Nolla & J. Tarrus (1982) 'The late Roman villa of Vilauba and its context', *Antiquaries Journal* 62.2: 245-82.

Keay, S.J. 1988 *Roman Spain* Berkeley & Los Angeles.

Keay, S.J. 1992 'The "Romanisation" of Turdetania', *Oxford Journal of Archaeology* 11: 275-315.

Keay, S., J. Creighton & J. Remesal Rodriguez 2000 *Celti (Penaflor)* Oxford.

Kehoe, D. 1990 'Pastoralism and agriculture', *JRA* 3: 386-98.

King, A. 1990 'The emergence of Romano-Celtic religion', *The Early Roman Empire in the West* ed. T. Blagg & M. Millett. Oxford: 220-39.

King, A. 1991 'Food production and consumption-meat', *Britain in the Roman Period: Recent Trends* ed. R.F.J. Jones. Sheffield: 15-20.

King, A. 1999 'Diet in the Roman world: a regional inter-site comparison of the mammal bones', *JRA* 12: 168-202.

Kooistra, L.I. 1996 *Borderland Farming: Possibilities and Limitation of Farming in the Roman Period and Early Middle Ages between the Rhine and Meuse* Assen.

Lafon, X. 2001 *Villa Maritima* Rome.

Laubenheimer, F. 1985 *La production des amphores en Gaule narbonnaise* Paris.

Lauffray, J., J. Schreyeck & N. Dupre, 1973 'Les etablissements et les villas gallo-romains de Lalonquette', *Gallia* 31: 123-55.

Laurence, R. 1999 *The Roads of Roman Italy* London.

Lefebvre, L. 1975 *Les sculptures gallo-romaines du Musee d'Arlon* Arlon.

Lefebre, L. 1980 *La vie quotidienne dans le vicus d'Arlon durant les trois premiers siècles de notre ère* Arlon.

Lehmann, K. 1991 *Thomas Jefferson: American Humanist* Charlottesville, VA.

Leone, M. 1984 'Interpreting ideology in historical archaeology: using the rules of perspective in the William Paca Garden in Annapolis, Maryland', *Ideology, Power, and Prehistory* ed. D. Miller & C. Tilley. Cambridge: 25-35.

Leroy, M., M. Mangin, H. Laurent, M. Bezzoula & B. Raissouni 2000 'La sidérugie dans l'est de la Gaule', *Gallia* 57: 1-158.

Leveau, Ph. 1984 *Caesarea de Maurétanie: une ville romaine et ses campagnes* Rome.

Leveau, P., P. Sillieres & J-P. Vallet 1993 *Campagnes de la Méditerranée romaine* Paris.

Lloyd, J. 1991 'Farming the highlands: Samnium and Arcadia in the Hellenistic and Early Roman periods', *Roman Landscapes* ed. G. Barker & J. Lloyd. London: 180-93.

Lugli, G. 1926 'La villa sabina di Orazio', *Mont. Ant.* 31: 457-598.

MacDonald, W.L. & J.A. Pinto 1995 *Hadrian's Villa and its Legacy* New Haven.

MacKendrick, P. 1972 *Roman France* New York.

MacKinnon, M.R. 2002 *The Excavations of San Giovanni di Ruoti*, vol. 3: *The Faunal and Plant Remains* Toronto.

Magrini, C. 1997 'Il territorio di Aquileia tra tardoantico e altomedioevo', *Archeologia Medievale* 24: 155-71.

Maiuri, A. 1931 *La villa dei Misteri* Rome.

Matthews, K.J. 1996 'Immaterial culture: invisible peasants and consumer subcultures in north-west Britannia', *TRAC 96*: 120-32.

Mattingly, D.J. 1985 'Olive oil production in Roman Tripolitania', *Town and Country in Roman Tripolitania* Oxford: 27-46.

Mattingly, D.J. 1989 'Olive cultivation and the Albertini tablets', *L'Africa romana* 6: 403-15.

Mattingly, D.J. 1989a 'Field survey in the Libyan Valleys', *JRA* 2: 275-280.

Mattingly, D.J. 1994 *Tripolitania* Ann Arbor.

Mattingly, D.J. 1997 'Africa: a landscape of opportunity', *Dialogues of Roman Imperialism* ed. D.J. Mattingly. Portsmouth, RI: 117-42.

Mattingly, D.J. & J.W. Hayes 1992 'Nador and fortified farms in North Africa', *JRA* 5: 408-16.

Maune, S. 2000 'La question des premières installations rurales italiennes en Gaule transalpine', *Gallia* 57: 231-60.

McCann, A.M. et al. 1987 *The Roman Port and Fishery of Cosa* Princeton.

Meiggs, R. 1982 *Trees and Timbers in the Ancient Mediterranean World* Oxford.

Mermet, C. 1993 'La sanctuaire gallo-romain de Châteauneuf (Savoie)', *Gallia* 50: 95-138

Millet, M. 1990 *The Romanization of Britain* Cambridge.

Millet, M. 1991 'Pottery: population or supply patterns? The Ager Tarraconensis Approach', *Roman Landscapes* ed. G. Barker & J. Lloyd. London: 18-26.

Miret, M., J. Sanmarti & J. Santacana 1991 'From indigenous structures to the Roman world: models for the occupation of central coastal Catalunya', *Roman Landscapes* ed. G. Barker & J. Lloyd. London: 47-53.

Moore, J.P. 2002 'Straight from the bottle: rural life in Roman Africa', *AJA* 106: 313-15.

Moreland, J. 'Wilderness, wasteland, depopulation and the end of the Roman empire', *The Accordia Research Papers* 4: 89-110.

Moreland, J. & M. Pluciennik 1991 'Excavations at Casale San Donato Castelnuovo di Farfa (RI) 1990', *Archeologia medievale* 18: 477-90.

Moreland, J. et al. 1993 'Excavations at Casale San Donato, Castelnuovo di Farfa (RI), Lazio 1992', *Archeologia Medievale* 20: 185-228.

Motta, L. 1997 'I paesaggi di Volterra nel tardantico', *Archeologia Medievale* 24: 245-67.

Nagle, D.B. 1976 'The Etruscan journey of Tiberius Gracchus', *Historia* 25: 487-9.

Olesti Vila, O. 1997 'El origen de las *villae* romanas en Cataluña', *AEspA* 70: 71-90.

Orejas, A. & F.J. Sanchez-Palencia 2002 'Mines: territorial organization and social structure in Roman Iberia', *AJA* 106: 581-99.

Pailler, J-M. 1987 'Montmaurin: a Garden Villa', *Ancient Roman Gardens* ed. E. Macdougall. Dumbarton Oaks: 207-21.

Painter, K. 1999 'Natives, Romans and Christians at Uley? Questions of continuity of use of sacred sites', *JRA* 12: 694-702.

Palmer, R. 1996 'Air photo interpretation and the Lincolnshire Fenland', *Landscape History* 18: 5-16.

Parslow, C.C. 1995 *Rediscovering Antiquity* Cambridge.

Pasquinucci, M. & S. Menchelli 1999 'The landscape and economy of the territories of *Pisae* and *Volaterrae* (coastal North Etruria)', *JRA* 12: 123-41.

Peacock, D. 1977 'Recent discoveries of Roman amphora kilns in Italy', *Antiquaries Journal* 57: 262-9.

Peacock, D. 1982 *Pottery in the Roman World* London.

Percival, J. 1976 *The Roman Villa* Berkeley & Los Angeles.

Petts, D. 1996 'Elite settlements in the Roman and sub-Roman period', *TRAC 96:* 101-12.

Piganiol, A. 1962 *Les documents cadastraux de la colonie romaine d'Orange* Paris.

Ponsich, M. 1974-87 *L'implantation rurale antique sur le Bas-Guadalquivir* Paris.

Ponsich, M. 1998 'The rural economy of western Baetica', *The Archaeology of Early Roman Baetica* ed. S. Keay. Portsmouth, RI: 171-82.

Potter, T.W. 1979 *The Changing Landscape of South Etruria* London.

Potter, T.W. 1981 'Marshland and drainage in the classical world', *The evolution of marshland landscapes* R.T. Rowley: 1-19.

Potter, T.W. 1989 'Recent work on the Roman Fens of eastern England and the question of imperial estates', *JRA* 2: 267-74.

Potter, T.W. 1999 'Roman wetlands archaeology in Britain: the Severn Estuary and the Fens compared', *JRA* 12: 689-93.

Potter, T.W. & K.M. Dunbabin 1979 'A Roman villa at Crocicchie, Via Clodia', *PBSR* 47: 19-26.

Potter, T.W. & A.C. King eds 1997 *Excavations at the Mola di Monte Gelato: a Roman and Medieval Settlement in South Etruria* London.

Prevosti, M. 1991 'The establishment of the villa system in the Maresme (Catalonia) and its development in the Roman period', *Roman Landscapes* ed. G. Barker & J. Lloyd: 135-41.

Pucci, P. 1973 'La produzione della ceramica aretina, Note sull' "industria" nella prima età imperiale romana', *Dial. Arch.* 7: 255-93.

Purcell, N. 1987 'Town in country and country in town', *Ancient Roman Gardens* ed. E. MacDoughall. Dumbarton Oaks: 187-203.

Rathbone, D.W. 1981 'The development of agriculture in the "Ager Cosanus" during the Roman Republic: problems of evidence and interpretation', *JRS* 71: 10-23.

Reddé, M. 1995 'Les agglomérations secondaires en Gaule', *JRA* 8: 511-13.

Remesal Rodriguez, J. 1998 'Baetican olive oil and the Roman economy', *The Archaeology of Early Roman Baetica* ed. S. Keay. Portsmouth, RI: 183-200.

Richardson, J.E. 1996 'Economy and ritual: the use of animal bone in the interpretation of the Iron Age to Roman cultural transition', *TRAC 96*: 82-90.

Riley, D.N. 1987 *Air Photography and Archaeology* London.

Rippengal, R. 1993 ' "Villas as a key to social structures"? Some comments on recent approaches to the Romano-British villa and some suggestions toward an alternative', *TRAC 1*: 79-101.

Rippon, S. 1997 *The Severn estuary: landscape evolution and wetland reclamation* Leicester.

Rippon, S. 2000 *The Transformation of Coastal Wetlands* Oxford.

Rivet, A.L.F. 1969 *The Roman Villa in Britain* New York.

Roberto, C., J. Plambeck & A. Small 'The chronology of the sites of the Roman period around San Giovanni: methods of analysis and conclusions', *Archaeological Field Survey in Britain and Abroad* ed. S. Macready & F.H. Thompson. London: 136-45.

Romizzi, L. 2001 *Ville d'Otium dell'Italia antica* Naples.

Rorison, M. 2001 *Vici in Roman Gaul* Oxford.

Rossiter, J.J. 1981 'Wine and oil processing at Roman farms in Italy', *Phoenix* 35: 345-62.

Rossiter, J.J. 1988 'Villas vandales: le *suburbium* de Carthage au début du vi siècle de notre ère', *113e Congrès national des sociétés savants, Strasbourg, 1988, IVe Colloque sur l'histoire et l'archéologie de l'Afrique du Nord,* t.1: 221-7.

Rossiter, J.J. 2000 'Interpreting Roman villas', *JRA* 13: 572-7.

Rostovtzeff, M. 1926 *Social and Economic History of the Roman World* Oxford.

Rushforth, A. 1999 'From periphery to core in late Antique Mauretania', *TRAC 99*: 91-103.

Schmiedt, G. 1970 *Atlante aerofotografico degli sedi umane in Italia* Florence.

Scott, E. 1993 *A Gazetteer of Roman Villas in Britain* Leicester.

Scott, J.S. 1985 *Weapons of the Weak* New Haven.

Scott, S. 1993 'A theoretical framework for the study of Roman-British villa mosaics', *TRAC 1*: 103-14.

Scott, S. 1994 'Patterns of movement: architectural design and visual planning in the Romano-British villa' in *Meaningful Architecture: Social Interpretation of Buildings* ed. M. Locock. Aldershot: 86-98.

Settis, S. ed. 1983 *Misurare la terra: centuriazione e coloni nel mondo romano* Modena.

Sjostrom, I. 1993 *Tripolitiania in Transition: Late Roman to Early Islamic Settlement* Aldershot.

Small, A.M. 1991 'Late Roman rural settlement in Basilicata and Western Apulia', *Roman Landscapes* ed. G. Barker & J. Lloyd. London: 204-22.

Small, A.M and R.J. Buck eds *The Excavations at San Giovanni di Ruoti: The Villas and their Environment* vol. 1 Toronto and London.

Smith, J.T.S. 1997 *Roman Villas: A Study in Social Structure* London.

Soren, D. & N. 1999 *A Roman Villa and a Late Roman Infant Cemetery: Excavations at Poggio Gramignano Lugnano in Teverina* Rome.

Staffa, A. 2000 'Le campagne Abruzzesi fra tarda antichità ed altomedioevo', *Arch. Med.* 27: 47-99.

Steele, G. 1983: 'The analysis of the animal remains from the late Roman middens at San Giovanni di Ruoti', *Lo Scavo di San Giovanni di Ruoti ed il Periodo Tardoantico in Basilicata* ed. M. Gualtieri et al.: 75-84.

Sternini, M., ed. 2000 *La villa romana di Cottanello* Bari.

Stirling, E. 'Divinities and heroes in the age of Ausonis: a late-antique villa and sculptural collection at Saint-Georges-de-Montagne (Gironde)', *Rev. Arch.* 103-41.

Stirling, E. 1999 'The sculptures of the villa of El Ruedo', *JRA* 12: 669-71.

Stone, D.L. 1997 *The Development of an Imperial Territory: Romans, Africans, and the Transformation of the Rural Landscape of Tunisia* Ph.D. Diss. University of Michigan. Ann Arbor.

Stone, D.L. 2000 'Society and economy in North Africa', *JRA* 13: 721-4.

Strutt, K. 1999 'Use of a GIS for regional archaeological analysis: application of computer-based techniques to Iron Age and Roman settlement distribution in north- west Portugal', *TRAC 99*: 118-41.

Taylor, J. 2000 'Stonea in its Fenland context: moving beyond an imperial estate', *JRA* 13: 647-58.

Tchernia, A. 1986 *Le vin de l'Italie romaine* Rome.

Terrenato, N. 2001 'The Auditorium site in Rome and the origins of the villa', *JRA* 14: 5-32.

Thomas, R. & A. Wilson 1994 'Water supply for Roman farms in Latium and South Etruria', *PBSR* 62: 139-98.

Tomlin, R.S.O. 1996 'A five-acre wood in Roman Kent', *Interpreting Roman London* ed. J. Bird, M. Hassall & H. Sheldon. Oxford.

Tozzi, P. & M. Harari 1984 *Eraclea Veneta* Parma.

Traina, G. 1988 *Paludi e bonifiche del mondo antico* Rome.

Tyers, P. 1996 *Roman Pottery in Britain* London.

Van der Veen, M. 1992 *Crop Husbandry Regimes: An Archaeobotanical Study of Farming in Northern England 1000 BC-AD 500* Sheffield.

Van Dommelen, P. 1993 'Roman peasants and rural organization in Central Italy: an archaeological perspective', *TRAC* 1: 167-86.

Van Ossel, P. 1992 *Etablissements ruraux de l'Antiquité tardive dans le nord de la Gaule* Paris.

Van Ossel, P. & P. Ouzoulias 2000 'Rural settlement economy in Northern Gaul in the Late Empire: overview and assessment', *JRA* 13: 133-53.

Vaquerizo Gil, D. & J.R. Carillo Diaz-Pines 1995 'The Roman villa of El Ruedo (Almedinilla, Corduba)', *JRA* 8: 121-60.

Vita-Finzi, C., 1969 *The Mediterranean Valleys* Cambridge.

Volpe, G 1992 *Paesaggio agrario, produzione e scambi nell'Apulia tardoantica* San Marino.

Volpe, G., ed. 1998 *San Giusto: La villa, le ecclesie. Scavi archeologici nel sito rurale di San Giusto Lucera* Bari.

Wagstaff, J.M. 1981 'Buried assumptions: some problems in the inter-

pretation of the "Younger Fill" raised by recent data from Greece',
J. Arch. Science 8: 257-64.

Webster, J. 1997. 'A negotiated syncretism: readings on the development of Romano-Celtic religion', *Dialogues in Roman Imperialism*
ed. D.J. Mattingly. Portsmouth, RI: 165-84.

Webster, J. 2001 'Creolizing the Roman provinces', *AJA* 105: 209-25.

White, R.H. & P.M. van Leusen 1996 'Aspects of Romanization in the
Wroxeter hinterland', *TRAC 96*: 133-43.

White, K.D. 1970 *Roman Farming* London.

Whittaker, C.R. ed. 1988 *Pastoral Economies in Classical Antiquity*
Cambridge.

Widrig, W. 1987 'Land use at the Via Gabina villas', *Ancient Roman
Villa Gardens* ed. E. Macdougall. Dumbarton Oaks: 223-60.

Wightman, E. 1970 *Roman Trier and the Treveri* London.

Wightman, E. 1978 'North-eastern Gaul in late Antiquity: the testi-
mony of settlement patterns in an age of transition', *Ber. ROB* 28:
241-50.

Wightman, E. 1985 *Gallia Belgica* Berkeley & Los Angeles.

Willems, W.J.H. 1981-84 *Romans and Batavians: A Regional Study in
the Dutch Eastern River Area* Amsterdam.

Willey, G. & J. Sabloff 1980 *A History of American Archaeology* San
Francisco.

Williams, H.M.R. 1997 'The Ancient Monument in Romano-British
Ritual Practices', *TRAC 97*: 72-86.

Williamson, T.M. 1984 'The Roman countryside: settlement and agriculture in N.W. Essex', *Britannia* 15: 225-30.

Wills, G. 1984 *Cincinnatus: George Washington and the Enlightenment*
New York.

Wilson, R.J.A. 1990 *Sicily under the Roman Empire* Warminster.

Witcher, R. 1997 'Roman roads: phenomenological perspectives on
roads in the landscape', *TRAC 97*: 60-70.

Woodward, A. & P. Leach 1993 *The Uley Shrines: Excavations of a
Ritual Complex on West Hill, Uley, Gloucestershire: 1997-9* London.

Woolf, G. 1998 *Becoming Roman: The Origins of Provincial Civilization
in Gaul* Cambridge.

Woolf, G. 2000 'The religious history of the northwest provinces', *JRA*
13: 615-30.

Index

Index